Second Grade
ESSENTIALS
for Social Studies

by Carole Marsh

REPRODUCIBLE!

Dear Teachers,

Have you ever wished you had everything you needed to teach social studies in one easy-to-use resource? Now you have it in *Second Grade Essentials for Social Studies*. Even in second grade, students are expected to learn a lot! This book will help you meet essential state standards with age-appropriate activities in a fun, attractive, and interesting style!

In addition to more than 100 reproducible activity pages, this book offers even more hands-on learning opportunities with templates, graphic organizers, writing prompts, project-based learning ideas, and vocabulary cards with definitions. The writing prompts and vocabulary cards are designed so you can cut them out individually. You can mix and match these "extras" to topics you are studying, to activity pages in the book, or use them on their own.

What is my goal with this book? I want to make your life easier as you introduce your students to the social studies topics and skills they absolutely need to know. I am confident this book accomplishes exactly that!

From my desk to yours,

Your Second Grade Essentials are already attractive and fun (in addition to educational, of course), but you can customize them to make them colorful and unique!

Copy Writing Prompts and Vocabulary Cards onto colored paper. Choose colors that match your classroom decorative theme, a theme for social studies materials, or use an assortment of colors. Or, as an alternative, copy them onto white paper, and use your markers, highlighters, stickers, and glitter-glue to add personalization and pizzazz to the borders. Either way, laminate them so they last!

P.S. I would LOVE to see what you come up with! Connect with me at Gallopade on Facebook or Pinterest.

Table of Contents

Foundations

Geography

History

Government

Civics

Economics

Appendix

Social Studies Reference Skills

As you study social studies, you will need tools to help you find information about people, places, and events.

Those tools are known as **reference resources**.

Some reference resources you can use include:

- **atlas:** a book of maps

- **biography:** the story of someone's life

- **encyclopedia:** a book or set of books with information on many subjects

- **textbook:** a book for students to use to study a subject at school

- **website:** a place on the internet with digital information about a subject

Use the Word Bank to complete the sentences.

1. Adyson found a book in the library about the life of Abraham Lincoln. She found a _____.

2. Tyler used his computer to find his state's symbols. He used a _____.

3. Kylie's teacher gave each student a book to use for social studies. Kylie has a _____.

4. Maggie went to the library. She needed to find information on many different subjects. Maggie used an _____.

5. Deon needed a map of every state. He used an _____.

Word Bank

encyclopedia
textbook
atlas
website
biography

Primary Sources

One way to learn about the past is from primary sources. Primary sources are records of events as they are first described. Primary sources are usually recorded by people who saw or participated in the event. Artifacts such as tools, clothing, or food that people used in the past are also primary sources.

 artifact: an object used by people in the past

These are examples of primary sources:

maps   diaries   journals   interviews with a witness

photographs   artifacts

speeches   historical documents

On April 11, 1965, a tornado hit a city in the United States.
Put a ✓ by the items that are primary sources about the event.

_____ 1. a photograph of the tornado

_____ 2. a book about tornadoes, hurricanes, and other dangerous weather

_____ 3. a journal entry written by a girl whose house was destroyed by the tornado

_____ 4. a speech made by the mayor about damage from the tornado

_____ 5. a hospital document listing how many people in the community were injured by the tornado

COMMUNITIES CHANGE

A **community** is a group of people living together in one place.

Your neighborhood and town, are examples of communities.

What was your community like 100 years ago? It was probably very different than it is today. That is because communities change a lot over the years! Primary sources, such as artifacts, maps, and photographs can be used to show how a community changes over time. You might see that areas of your community like these have changed over time:

businesses   **employment**   **technology**   **religion**   **recreation**

architecture   **education**   **physical features**   **transportation**

Fill in the blanks with the correct words from the Word Bank.

1. Your local _____ has a history all its own! You can learn about your local community by studying _____ sources.

2. Primary sources are _____ of events as they are first described—usually by someone who saw or participated in the event.

3. When you examine primary sources such as _____, maps, and photographs, you can see how your community has changed over time.

Word Bank

primary
artifacts
records
community

PHOTOGRAPHS SHOW CHANGE

Photographs help us see how daily life has changed over time.

Past (1930)

Washing clothes by hand was a difficult chore.

Today

Washing machines make washing clothes much easier. Just push a button!

Look at the photographs and answer the questions.

Past (1909): These children are working at a clothing factory.

Today: These children are at school.

1. What was life like for children in the past? _____

_____

2. How is life different for children today? _____

_____

3. Do the children's clothes in 1909 look like children's clothes today? _____

USING A CALENDAR

A calendar helps us measure time. A calendar helps us know when something happened in the past. It also helps us know when something will happen in the future.

We can measure days, weeks, months, and years on a calendar by counting. When we count, we do not count the starting day, week, month, or year.

FOR EXAMPLE:

Imagine today is Thursday, January 10. To find out what day it will be in three days, count forward. (Do not count the starting day.)
In three days, the day will be

Sunday, January 13

YOUR TURN:

• To find out what day it was four days ago, count backward. Try it!
• Four days ago, the day was

_____

January

Sunday	Monday	Tuesday	Wednesday	Thursday	Friday	Saturday
		1	2	3	4	5
4 6	3 7	2 8	1 9	10 Today	1 11	2 12
3 13	14	15	16	17	18	19
20	21	22	23	24	25	26
27	28	29	30	31		

Look at the calendar. Count the days from "today" to each event on the calendar. Fill in the blanks.

1. The soccer game was _____ days ago.

2. The doctor's appointment is _____ days from today.

3. Martin Luther King Jr. Day is _____ days from today.

January

Sunday	Monday	Tuesday	Wednesday	Thursday	Friday	Saturday
		1	2	3	4	5 Soccer game
6	7	8	9	10 Today	11	12
13	14 MLK Day	15	16	17 Doctor appt.	18	19
20	21	22	23	24	25	26
27	28	29	30	31		

Days and Weeks

Time can be shown on a calendar.

Calendars show days, weeks, months, and years.

There are seven days in a week. The days of the week are Sunday, Monday, Tuesday, Wednesday, Thursday, Friday, and Saturday. The first day of the week is Sunday. The last day of the week is Saturday. After Saturday, the week starts over again on Sunday!

Write the first three letters of the missing days of the week. Then, list weeks of the month.

This is a calendar:
Days and Weeks of May

Week 1 ➡

➡

➡

➡

	MON			THU		
1	2	3	4	5	6	7
8	9	10	11	12	13	14
15	16	17	18	19	20	21
22	23	24	25	26	27	28
29	30	31				

What day comes...

after Tuesday? _____   before Tuesday? _____

before Friday? _____   after Saturday? _____

Find each date listed below on the calendar above. Write the day of the week and week of the month.

Date:	Day of the week:	Week of the month:
• May 3	_____	_____
• May 13	_____	_____
• May 18	_____	_____

Months of the Year

There are 12 **months** in a year. January is the first month. December is the last month. After December, a new year begins in January!

On many calendars, each page of a calendar shows one month of the year.

A year has 12 months. Most years have 365 days. Some years, called **leap years**, have 366 days!

January

February

March

April

May

June

July

August

September

October

November

December

List the months of the year in order.

1. _____

2. _____

3. _____

4. _____

5. _____

6. _____

7. _____

8. _____

9. _____

10. _____

11. _____

12. _____

Answer the questions.

How many months are in one year? _____

How many months are in two years? _____

Write About It:

Which month were you born in?

_____

What do you like most about that month?

_____

_____

Timelines Show Events

Time can be shown on a **timeline**. A timeline shows events in the order they happened. Because the events are in **chronological order**, it is easy to see which events happened before or after other events.

 **WORD TO KNOW!** **chronological order:** the order in which events happened

This is a timeline:

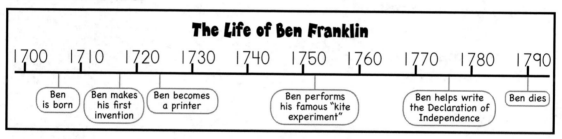

The Life of Ben Franklin

1700   1710   1720   1730   1740   1750   1760   1770   1780   1790

Ben is born | Ben makes his first invention | Ben becomes a printer | Ben performs his famous "kite experiment" | Ben helps write the Declaration of Independence | Ben dies

Use the timeline to answer the questions.

1. Which event on the timeline happened first? _____

2. Which event on the timeline happened last? _____

3. What did Ben Franklin do in 1723? _____

Draw lines to add the missing events to the timeline in chronological order.
The Life of Neil Armstrong

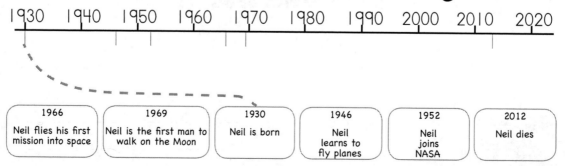

1930   1940   1950   1960   1970   1980   1990   2000   2010   2020

| 1966 | 1969 | 1930 | 1946 | 1952 | 2012 |
| Neil flies his first mission into space | Neil is the first man to walk on the Moon | Neil is born | Neil learns to fly planes | Neil joins NASA | Neil dies |

MAPS AND GLOBES

We can look at Earth on maps and globes.
Maps and globes help people study Earth.

- A **globe** is a round model of Earth.
- A **map** is a drawing that shows what places look like from above.

Maps and globes can be used to locate features on Earth's surface.
Features include land and water.

 **WORD TO KNOW!**   land: the solid surface of Earth

**The globe shows land and water on Earth.
Color the land green. Color the water blue.**

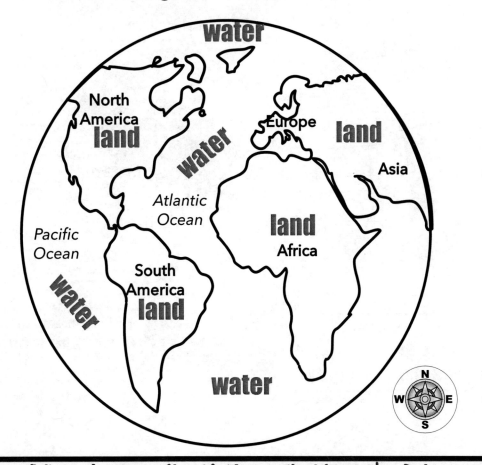

Map Tools

People who make maps include tools to help us read the map. These tools help us find where things are located and learn what places are like.

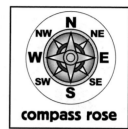

compass rose

- A **map title** tells what type of information a map shows.

- A **map key** is a list of symbols used on a map. The symbols represent objects and places. The map key tells what each symbol stands for.

- A **compass rose** is a symbol that shows directions (north, south, east, west). These directions are called **cardinal directions**. A compass rose can also have intermediate directions (northeast, northwest, southeast, and southwest). **Intermediate directions** are the directions between north, south, east, and west.

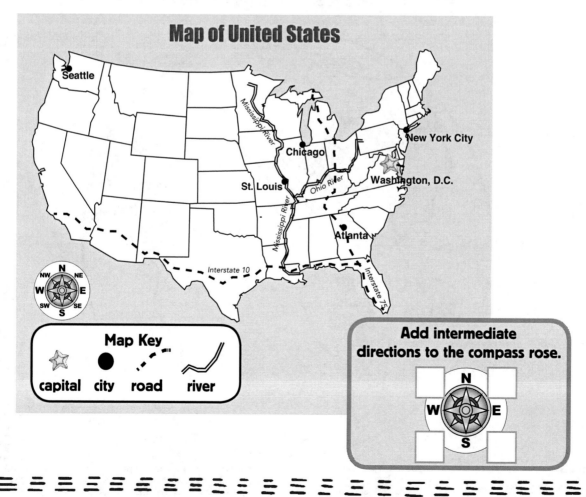

Map Grids

We use maps to find places. Most maps have a grid. A **map grid** is the lines on a map. These lines run from the top of the map to the bottom, and from the left side of the map to the right side. The lines cross and make boxes on the map. Each box can be identified with a letter and a number.

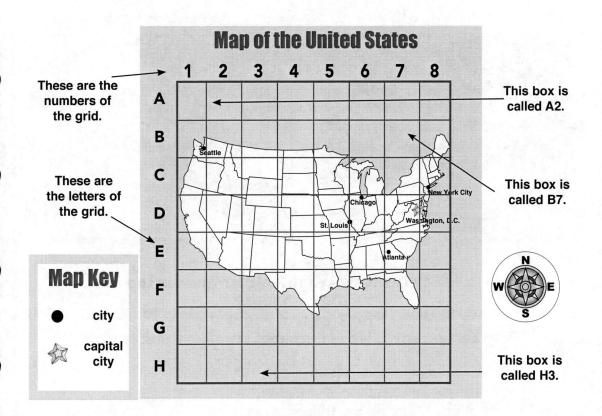

Map of the United States

These are the numbers of the grid.

These are the letters of the grid.

This box is called A2.

This box is called B7.

This box is called H3.

Map Key

● city

☆ capital city

Use the map and map grid to answer the questions.

1. Which city is located in E7?   **Chicago   Atlanta   St. Louis**

2. What city is in C8? _____

3. What square contains Seattle? _____

4. Is our nation's capital north, south, east, or west of B7? _____

Maps Can Show Change

Maps can tell us a lot about daily life. They can also show how daily life changed over time.

These maps both show the same place at two different times. You can use them to learn how daily life has changed over time.

Miller Town in 1915

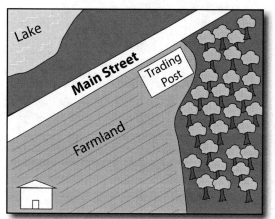

Miller Town today

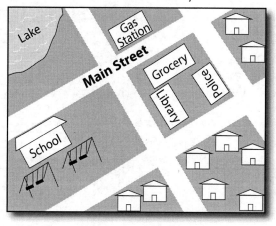

**Compare Miller Town today with Miller Town in the past.
How did it change?
Write T for True and F for False.
Then correct any false statements to make them true.**

_____ 1. People cut down the forests.

_____ 2. People built many houses to live in.

_____ 3. People changed the forest into farms.

_____ 4. More people live in the town today than in the past.

_____ 5. There are fewer roads today than in the past.

_____ 6. Today, people shop for food at the grocery store.

_____ 7. Today, children work on the farm instead of going to school.

_____ 8. Today, children have a playground to play on.

Identifying Continents

A continent is a large body of land on Earth.
Earth has seven continents.

Find each continent on the map:

- Color North America green.
- Color South America red.
- Color Australia orange.
- Color Antarctica black.

- Color Asia brown.
- Color Europe yellow.
- Color Africa purple.

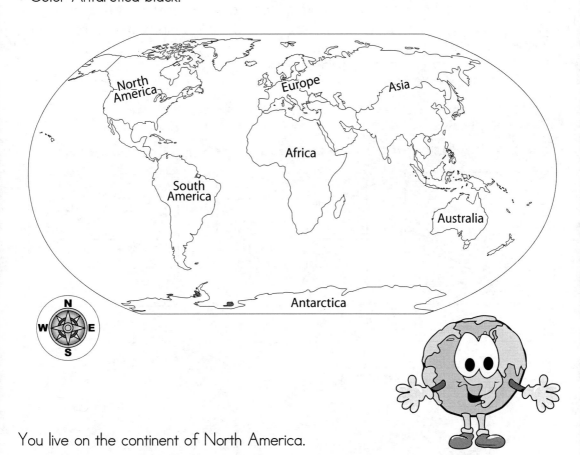

You live on the continent of North America.

Circle North America on the map above.

Maps Can Show Landforms

Landforms are the natural physical characteristics of land. Landforms include mountains, valleys, plateaus, and more. Maps often show where landforms are located.

We can use the information on maps to learn where landforms are located and what a place is like!

Examples of landforms:

mountain	hill	valley	plateau	island
an area of land, usually with steep sides that rise high above the land around it	a rounded area of land higher than the land around it, but not as high as a mountain	low land between mountains or hills	a large area of high, flat land	an area of land surrounded by water

Use the descriptions above to label each landform below.

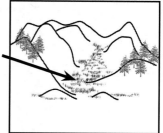

1. _____

2. _____

3. _____

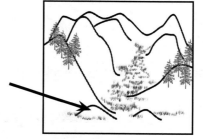

4. _____

5. _____

Landforms on a Map

We can use maps to learn about places. Then we can answer questions about the land and bodies of water nearby.

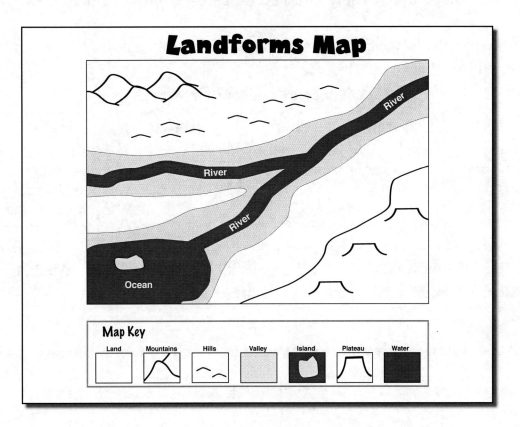

Complete the steps. Then answer the questions.

- Color the area that has mountains red.
- Color the valley blue.

- Color the area with hills yellow.
- Color the plateau area green.
- Color the island brown.

1. Which landform is closer to the valley?

_____ a) mountains _____ b) hills _____ c) plateaus

2. What landforms would you cross to travel from the island to the mountains?

_____

_____

Maps Can Show Water

Bodies of water are natural physical features of the landscape. Examples of bodies of water are creeks, ponds, lakes, rivers, and oceans. Maps often show where bodies of water are located.

We can use the information on maps to learn where things are located and what a place is like.

Examples of bodies of water:

lake	pond	river	stream	ocean
large body of water surrounded by land	small body of water surrounded by land	large, natural flow of water over land	small, natural flow of water over land	large body of salt water that covers nearly three-fourths of the Earth's surface

What is the difference between a pond and a lake? Size!

What is the difference between a creek and a river? Size!

Use the descriptions above to label each body of water below.

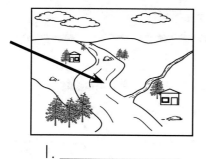

1. _____

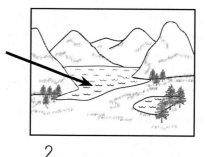

2. _____

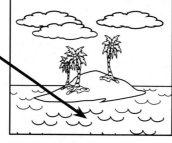

3. _____   4. _____   5. _____

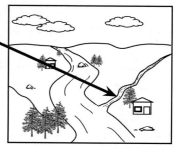

IDENTIFYING OCEANS

An ocean is a large body of water on Earth. Earth has five oceans.

Find each ocean on the map. Underline each ocean name.

- Write A on the Atlantic Ocean.
- Write P on the Pacific Ocean.
- Write I on the Indian Ocean.
- Write AR on the Arctic Ocean.
- Write S on the Southern Ocean.
- Color the continents green.

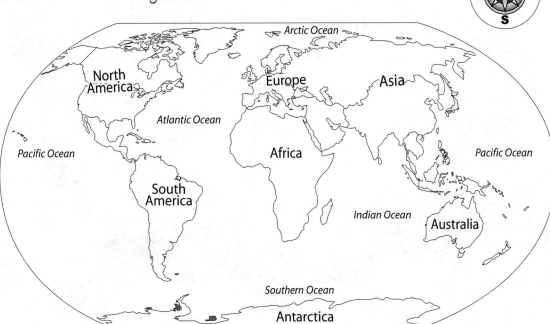

Answer the questions.

1. An ocean is a large body of _____.

    land   **water**   **people**

2. Earth has _____ oceans.

    7   **5**   **4**

Rivers, Lakes, and Mountains

We can use maps to locate rivers, lakes, and mountains.

1. Trace the United States in green.
2. Circle your state in red.
3. Color the Great Lakes blue.
4. Color the Appalachian Mountains and Rocky Mountains brown.
5. Trace the Mississippi River and Rio Grande in blue.

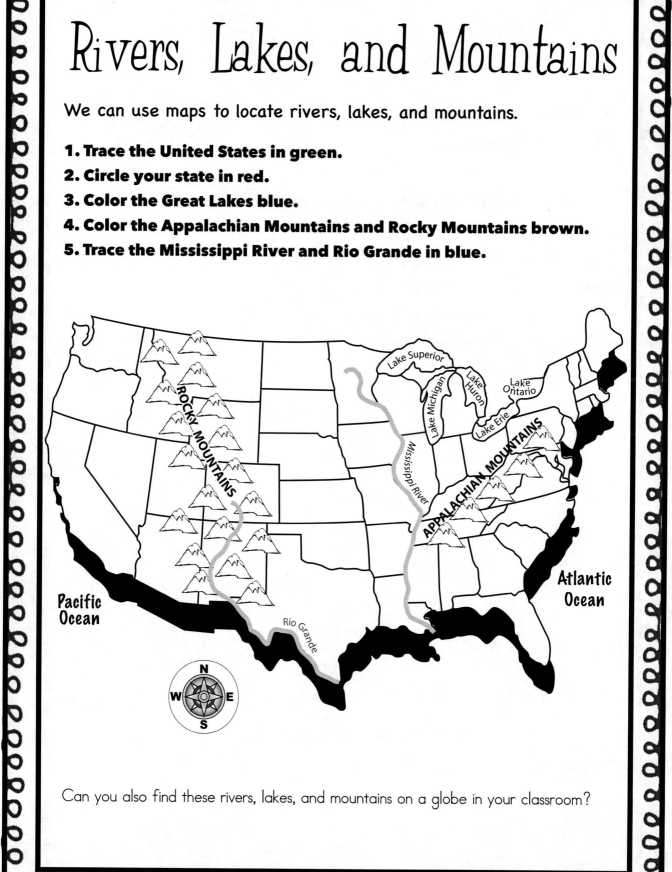

Can you also find these rivers, lakes, and mountains on a globe in your classroom?

BODIES OF WATER ON A MAP

We can use maps to learn about places. Then we can answer questions about the land and bodies of water nearby.

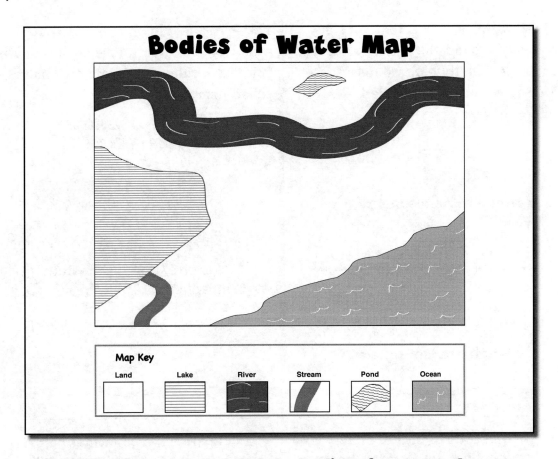

Complete the steps to label the bodies of water on the map. Then answer the questions.

- Write R on the river.
- Write S on the stream.

- Write O on the ocean.
- Write L on the lake.
- Write P on the pond.

1. Which body of water is closest to the ocean?

_____ a) pond   _____ b) creek   _____ c) river

2. Draw a new pond on the map between the ocean and the river.

   Show that it is a pond by using the symbol in the map key.

Imaginary Lines On Maps

Mapmakers created imaginary lines on Earth to help us find places. The lines run from top to bottom and from left to right.

The **equator** is a line that runs all the way around the middle of Earth. It divides Earth into two halves. These two halves are called **hemispheres.**

The **Prime Meridian** is a line that runs from the North Pole to the South Pole. It divides Earth into two halves, called hemispheres.

The poles can be thought of as the top and bottom of Earth.

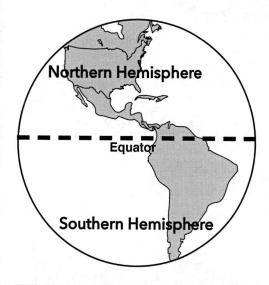

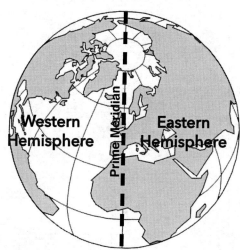

The equator divides Earth into the Northern Hemisphere and the Southern Hemisphere.

The Prime Meridian divides Earth into the Eastern Hemisphere and the Western Hemisphere.

Find the equator. Label it.
Find the Prime Meridian. Label it.

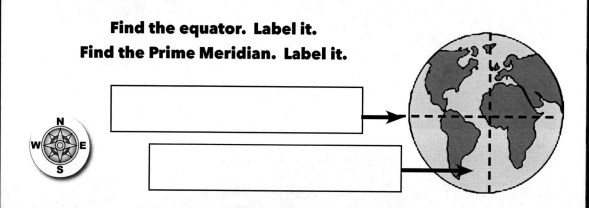

I Know My Hemispheres

1. **Draw a red line for the equator on the two maps.**
2. **Then label the hemisphere that is shaded gray on each map.**
   (Use the compass rose to help you.)

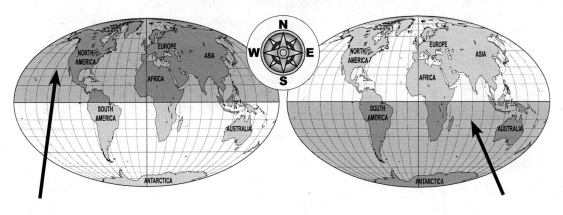

_____ Hemisphere   _____ Hemisphere

---

3. **Draw a blue line for the Prime Meridian on the two maps.**
4. **Then label the hemisphere that is shaded gray on each map.**
   (Use the compass rose to help you.)

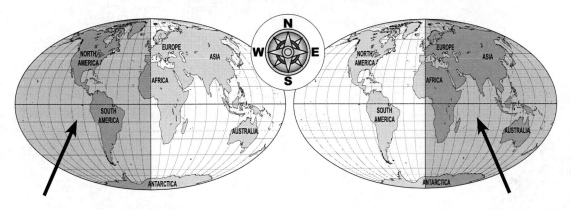

_____ Hemisphere   _____ Hemisphere

Physical Characteristics

Physical characteristics are natural parts of the land.
Physical characteristics include:

Landforms
natural land features

Examples include:

- mountains
- valleys
- plains
- plateaus
- hills

Climate
the typical weather in a place

Examples include:

- mild summers
- hot dry summers
- mild winters
- cold winters

Soil
the upper layer of earth where plants grow

Examples include:

- rocky soil
  (not good for crops)
- soil rich in nutrients
  (good for crops)
- sandy soil
  (not good for crops)

Water Sources
water that is available for people to use

Examples include:

- rainfall
- lakes
- rivers
- groundwater

Identify the physical characteristics in the picture.

1. What landforms do you see?

_____

2. What water sources do you see?

_____

3. What type of soil do you see?

_____

4. What examples of climate do you see?

_____

5. What is not a natural part of the physical environment?

_____

PHYSICAL CHARACTERISTICS AFFECT JOBS

Physical characteristics of places impact the work that people do. The physical environment provides resources for certain kinds of work. The physical environment also limits the kind of work people can do.

Where you live affects the work you do.
Some locations are better than other locations for certain types of work.

Here are some examples:

People who live on open land with rich soil might have jobs growing crops.

People who live near the ocean might have jobs building ships.

People who live in a desert climate would not have jobs fishing!

Match each job to a picture to identify the type of work people in each environment might do.

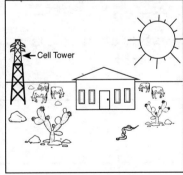 Cell Tower

1. _____   3. _____   5. _____

2. _____   4. _____   6. _____

JOBS

1. farmer   3. fisherman   5. ship builder

2. lumberjack   4. cell tower repairman   6. cattle farmer

Human Characteristics

Human characteristics are things people have added to a place and ways people have changed the environment. These include:

Buildings　　　　　　　**Where people live**

　　　Language　　　　　　　　　　**Roads**

Look at the pictures and complete the table.

Place 1

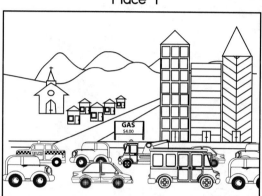

Place 2

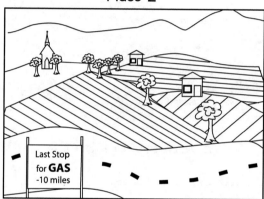

Describe human characteristics of both places and compare them.

Human Characteristics	Place 1	Place 2	Are they the same or different?
Population (do many people live here, or just a few?)			
Language			
Buildings			
Roads			

Human Characteristics Affect Jobs

Human characteristics of places affect the work people do. Population distribution—where people live—is an example.

RURAL AREA	• "the countryside" • area where few people live • people live farther apart

URBAN AREA	• "cities and towns" • area where lots of people live • people live closer together

Manufacturing jobs are jobs in which people make goods in factories. Factories need to be located where there are lots of workers. That means most factories are built in urban areas, and most manufacturing jobs are in urban areas!

Service jobs are jobs in which people provide a service. Examples of service jobs are waiter, doctor, and teacher. More services are needed where there are lots of people. That means there are more service jobs in urban areas!

For each picture or question, circle rural or urban.

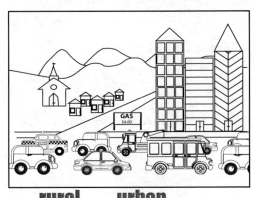

rural   urban

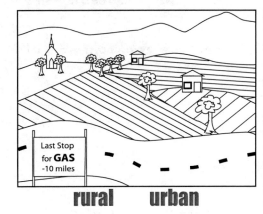

rural   urban

1. Which area is more likely to have factories that need lots of workers?   **rural**   **urban**

2. In which area are farmers most likely to live?   **rural**   **urban**

3. In which area are workers who provide services most likely to live?   **rural**   **urban**

People Modify the Environment

People depend on the **physical environment** around them to survive. People **modify** the physical environment to meet their basic needs.

For example, in the past and today, people cut down trees. Why?

To get wood to burn for fuel

To clear land for farming

To get wood to build houses

To clear land for roads and neighborhoods

All of these are good results of cutting down trees! But not all results are good. Some results are bad:

Burning trees pollutes the air.

Some animals lose their land and die.

Soil washes away more easily.

People have fewer trees to look at and enjoy.

Describe a result of each human change to the environment.

Dig a canal _____

Build a fence _____

Plant a vegetable garden _____

Discuss It

Compare answers to the activity above as a class.

Which results are good? Which results are bad? Can you think of more?

Consequences of Change

When people change the environment, things happen! Those results are called **consequences**. Consequences can be **positive** or **negative**.

WORD TO KNOW!

consequence: something that happens as a result of an action or event

Examples of Environmental Changes:

A dam is a barrier that blocks the flow of water. People modify the environment by building dams. People build dams to help control flooding. Dams also create lakes for recreation like boating or swimming. However, dams can destroy many animal homes.

People modify the environment by building highways. People build highways to improve transportation for cars and trucks. Highways help drivers get to their destinations faster and more safely. However, valuable farmland may be destroyed in order to build a highway.

Describe the positive and negative consequences of each change to the physical environment.

Modification	Positive Consequence	Negative Consequence
Dam		
Highway		

UNiqUe CULtUres

Culture describes the way of life for a group of people.
Culture includes:

| food | clothes | farming methods | language | buildings |

| beliefs | tools | holidays | family life | artistic expression |

 **WORD TO KNOW!** **culture:** the learned behavior of a group of people

Cultures develop in unique ways because people live in different **physical environments**. The physical environment influences how people meet their basic needs. That is why people eat, dress, and live differently depending on where they live.

For example, the ancient Egyptian culture lived near the Nile River in Africa. Their physical environment was a hot desert! Because of their environment, they met their basic needs in many unique ways:

 wrote their language using symbols called heiroglyphs

Ancient Egyptian Culture

made paper from papyrus plant that grew along the Nile River

wore linen clothing to keep cool in the heat

 used water from the Nile River to grow crops

 built temples out of large stones

The Iroquois were a Native American culture that developed long ago in North America. Match each part of the physical environment to how it influenced the Iroquois culture.

Iroquois physical environment

_____ 1. There were many rivers.

_____ 2. There were many forests.

_____ 3. Winter was very cold.

_____ 4. There were many animals in the forests.

Iroquois culture

A. The Iroquois often fished for food.

B. The Iroquois wore animal fur to stay warm.

C. The Iroquois built longhouses from wood.

D. The Iroquois often hunted for food.

Cultures Meet Needs and Wants

Cultural groups live in different **physical environments** around the world. Some places are hot. Some places are cold. Some places have good farmland. Some places do not. Some places are near rivers, lakes, and oceans. Some places are in deserts with no water. Because every environment is different, cultures meet their needs and wants in different ways.

 **physical environment:** the land, water, and climate of a place

Physical environment of China

China has flat, wet plains.

China has hot rainy summers. Floods happen often!

China has many silk worms.

Meeting needs and wants in China

Chinese people grow and eat a lot of rice. Rice grows well in China!

Some Chinese people build and live in houses on stilts to avoid floodwater.

Chinese people make and wear silk clothing.

Read about the Inuit people of the past.
Then, complete the sentences.

The Inuit people lived in the cold Arctic environment. The Arctic has lots of ice but not many trees. The Arctic does not have good soil for farming. But, the Arctic has lots of fish in the ocean. The Arctic is freezing many months of the year—BRRRRR! It's cold! There are many wild animals in the Arctic, including polar bears, caribou, seals, whales, and more! The Inuit used nature, like whale bone and wood, in their art.

1. The Inuit built homes made of blocks of _____.

2. The Inuit made clothing from animal fur. It helped them stay _____.

3. The Inuit ate lots of _____.

4. The Inuit created art from _____.

CULTURES CONNECT

Today, people do not meet all their needs on their own. People depend on each other. When people depend on each other, they are **interdependent**.

People around the world are dependent on each other. The world is becoming more and more interdependent all the time. People of various cultural groups around the world depend on each other for:

Goods   **Services**   **Natural Resources**   **Information**   **Ideas**

Put a ✓ next to the examples that show interdependence.

☐ Many people in France buy cars made in Italy.

☐ People around the world share information on the Internet.

☐ Americans borrowed the idea to build interstate highways from Germany.

☐ Some cultures do not trade because they make everything they need.

Because people are interdependent, cultural groups have more contact with each other. They work together, communicate, trade goods, and share information. As cultures interact, they share their ways of life. They share their **food, language,** and **customs**. They also borrow, adopt, and adapt new ideas.

Fill in the blanks from the Word Bank.

Today, the world is more _____.

That means people of many cultures interact and

_____. As they do, they

share their _____.

Word Bank

ways of life
work together
interdependent

CULTURES SHARE FOOD

Cultural groups around the world interact and share their ways of life. One part of their lives that they share is food!

Look at how we share, borrow, adopt, and adapt food from many different cultures!

Corn originally comes from the American Indian culture.
The first settlers in America borrowed corn from the American Indians.
Today, corn is an important part of many American foods!

Pizza is an Italian food!
Many Italian people moved to the United States in the 1900s.
They brought the recipe for pizza with them.
Today, Americans have adopted pizza as an American food, too!

French fries were first made in France. Today, many cultures eat French fries—not just the French! But, different cultures have adapted, or changed, how French fries are eaten. Americans often eat fries with ketchup.
Many Asian cultures eat fries with hot chili sauce or curry sauce.
Many European cultures eat fries with mayonnaise or vinegar.

Write T for True and F for False.
Then correct any false statements to make them true.

_____ 1. You have to travel to France to eat French fries.

_____ 2. All cultures eat French fries with ketchup.

_____ 3. People borrow, adopt, and adapt food from different cultures.

_____ 4. You must live in Italy to enjoy pizza.

_____ 5. You have to be from a culture to enjoy that culture's food.

_____ 6. Sharing culture allows us to enjoy many different foods.

_____ 7. When American Indians shared corn with the settlers, they were sharing their culture.

CULTURES SHARE LANGUAGES

People everywhere communicate. People learn to speak the language of their cultural group. When people from different cultural groups interact, they share their ways of life— that includes sharing language!

Many words in English today are borrowed from another languages.

French	Spanish	Italian	Chinese	Japanese
picnic	alligator	spaghetti	typhoon	karate
pork	taco	latte	chow mein	sushi
cream	burrito	biscuit	soy	tsunami
beef	tornado	cartoon	ketchup	teriyaki
menu	cafeteria	pasta	tea	karaoke

Many cultures around the world use English words, too!

English words used in other cultures:

weekend   hamburger   jeans   computer   notebook   jogging

Put a ✓ next to examples of sharing language.

_____ 1. You learn to say "hello" in many different languages.

_____ 2. You travel to Mexico and learn to speak some Spanish.

_____ 3. You shop at a local Chinese market and learn the names of many Chinese products.

_____ 4. You never learn to speak another language.

_____ 5. You have a Russian friend who teaches you many Russian words.

CULTURES SHARE CUSTOMS

Cultures around the world have many different customs!

WORD TO KNOW! 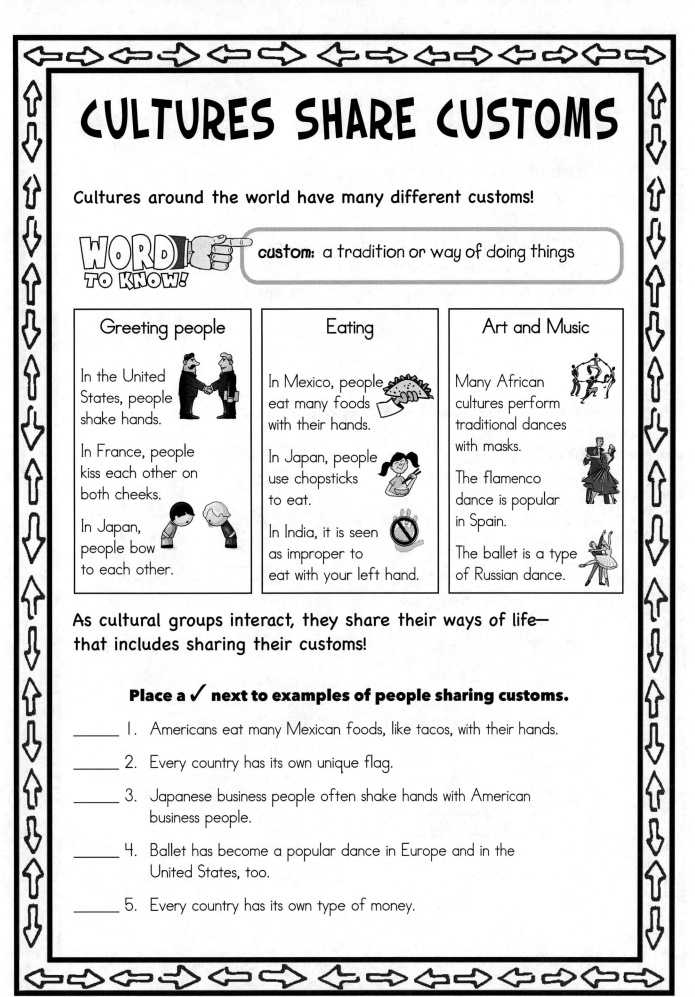 **custom:** a tradition or way of doing things

Greeting people

In the United States, people shake hands.

In France, people kiss each other on both cheeks.

In Japan, people bow to each other.

Eating

In Mexico, people eat many foods with their hands.

In Japan, people use chopsticks to eat.

In India, it is seen as improper to eat with your left hand.

Art and Music

Many African cultures perform traditional dances with masks.

The flamenco dance is popular in Spain.

The ballet is a type of Russian dance.

As cultural groups interact, they share their ways of life—that includes sharing their customs!

Place a ✓ next to examples of people sharing customs.

_____ 1. Americans eat many Mexican foods, like tacos, with their hands.

_____ 2. Every country has its own unique flag.

_____ 3. Japanese business people often shake hands with American business people.

_____ 4. Ballet has become a popular dance in Europe and in the United States, too.

_____ 5. Every country has its own type of money.

Communities Change

A **community** is a place where people live, work, and play. We all live in a community.

The way people live today is different from the way people lived long ago. Communities change over time for a variety of reasons. These are some of the ways communities change:

- transportation
- population
- buildings
- jobs

Circle the correct answer to the question below each graph.

Community Population

Is the population today more or less than long ago?

more   **less**

Computer Jobs

Do more people have computer jobs today or long ago?

today   **long ago**

Log Houses

Do people build more or fewer log houses today than long ago?

more   **fewer**

Car Transportation

Complete this graph by drawing bars to show how many people drive cars today compared to long ago.

Innovations and Inventions

Why do communities change? One reason is that people often come up with new ideas and ways of doing things.
These **innovations** often improve on methods of the past.

Innovations and inventions change how people live.
They can change how people work, communicate, and move from place to place.

 **innovation:** something new or different
population: the number of people living in a community

When innovations and inventions improve life in a community, more people move there. This causes the community population to grow!

For each part of daily life, write P by the picture that shows how it was done in the past. Write T by the picture that shows how innovations allow people to do it today.

place to live   **jobs to earn income**   **transportation**

 _____   _____    _____

 _____   _____   _____

Good jobs attract people to move to a new place.
Circle the reasons people need a good job.

to buy food   to buy clothing   to pay for a home

Communication

In United States history, important developments in **communication** changed the way people live and work!

communication: a way of sending information to people

People and businesses use **personal communication systems** to communicate one-to-one with each other. Methods that have been used over time in the United States include:

 Writing **letters** began long ago. Letters must be hand-delivered. Letters used to take weeks or months to arrive when sent across the country. Now they arrive in a few days!

1844 The **telegraph** sent messages called telegrams through signals along a wire from one telegraph station to another.

Communication

 1876 The **telephone** sent sounds over wire across long distances. People could have voice conversations with friends and family far away.

1990s–today **Cell phones** allow people to communicate anytime and anywhere. People can talk, text, and even send videos.

Number these innovations in the order people began to use them.

____ telegraph   ____ letters

____ telephone   ____ cell phone

Match each invention with its effect.

_____ 1. telegraph   A. People could have long-distance conversations.

_____ 2. telephone   B. Communication over wires replaced letters.

_____ 3. cell phone   C. People could communicate anytime and anywhere.

Mass Communication

When a message is delivered to many people at once, that is called **mass communication**.

Mass communication systems bring us news and entertainment. Mass communication systems that have been used over time in the United States include:

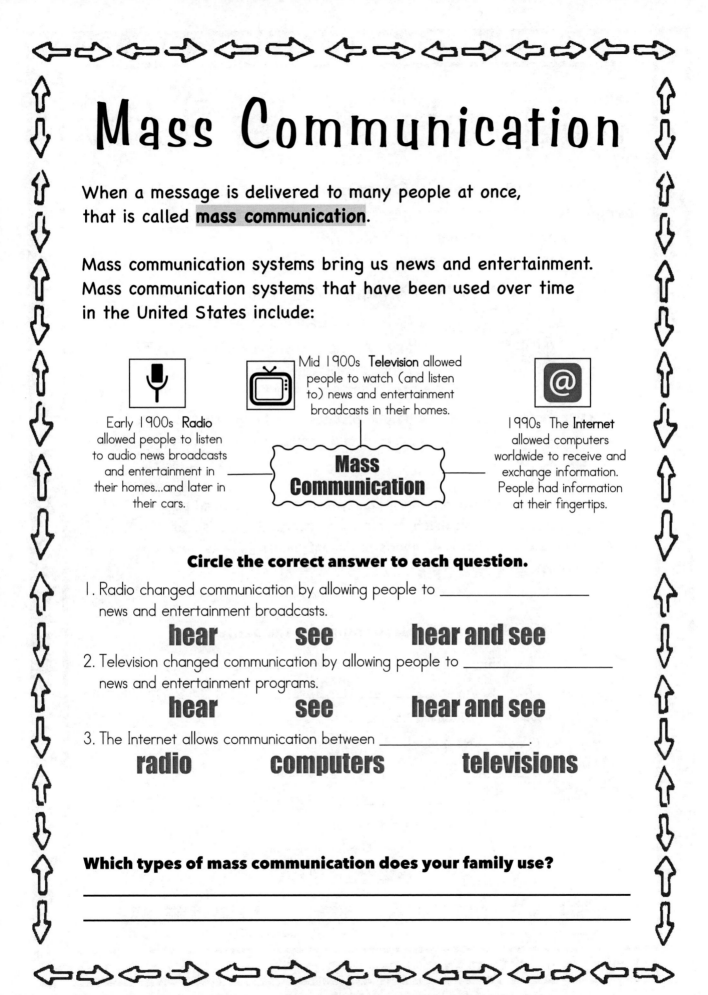

Early 1900s **Radio** allowed people to listen to audio news broadcasts and entertainment in their homes...and later in their cars.

Mid 1900s **Television** allowed people to watch (and listen to) news and entertainment broadcasts in their homes.

1990s The **Internet** allowed computers worldwide to receive and exchange information. People had information at their fingertips.

Mass Communication

Circle the correct answer to each question.

1. Radio changed communication by allowing people to _____ news and entertainment broadcasts.

   hear   **see**   **hear and see**

2. Television changed communication by allowing people to _____ news and entertainment programs.

   hear   **see**   **hear and see**

3. The Internet allows communication between _____.

   radio   **computers**   **televisions**

Which types of mass communication does your family use?

_____

_____

Transportation Shapes History

Important developments in **transportation** have changed the way people live and work. Transportation systems that have been used in the United States over time include:

horses → **covered wagons** → **steamboats** →
railroads → **automobiles** → **airplanes**

> **transportation:** a way of moving people and things from one place to another

- **Horses** and **covered wagons** helped pioneers settle the United States. The covered wagon was waterproof and carried all the supplies families needed to travel.

- **Steamboats** were invented in the early 1800s. They moved people and goods along rivers much faster than before. Farmers and merchants could ship their goods to distant places. Towns grew up along America's rivers!

Use the Word Bank to complete the sentences.

"My name is Joseph. I am a pioneer. I want to travel west! I need to buy a _____ to ride on my journey. My family is coming, too, so I need a _____ to carry our supplies! I am going to start a farm near a _____. I hear those new _____ can carry a farmer's goods to market in no time! I hope to make a lot of money!"

Word Bank

horse   **steamboats**   **river**   **covered wagon**

Transportation Keeps Moving!

Innovations continued in the world of transportation!

Railroads began to be built in the early 1800s.
Trains could travel four times as fast as a steamboat!
Railroads helped manufacturing grow. All kinds of
goods could be shipped anywhere they were needed.

Automobiles arrived in the early 1900s.
People had freedom to go wherever they wanted to go.
They could travel to jobs far from their homes.

Airplanes started flying in the early 1900s.
Airplanes changed the world! People and goods could
now be transported around the world in less than
a day.

New inventions lead to CHANGE!

**Write each transportation method from the Word Bank
in the correct section of the Venn diagram.**

Transportation Past and Present

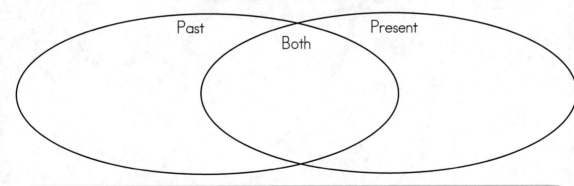

Past   Both   Present

Word Bank

**airplanes   horses   steamboats   railroads
covered wagons   automobiles**

AMERICAN INDIANS

American Indians lived in North America long before European explorers discovered the land. In fact, American Indians have lived throughout North America for thousands of years.

- The **Iroquois** lived in the **Eastern Woodlands** region.
- The **Cherokee** lived in the **Southeast** region.
- The **Lakota** lived in the **Plains** region.
- The **Pueblo** peoples lived in the **Southwest** region.
- The **Nez Perce** lived in the **West** region.

region: places that have common (the same) characteristics

Color each of the five labeled regions a different color.

Then color the boxes in the map legend to match the colors you used on the map.

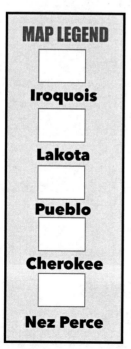

MAP LEGEND

Iroquois

Lakota

Pueblo

Cherokee

Nez Perce

INDIAN ENVIRONMENTS

The regions where American Indians lived had different environments.

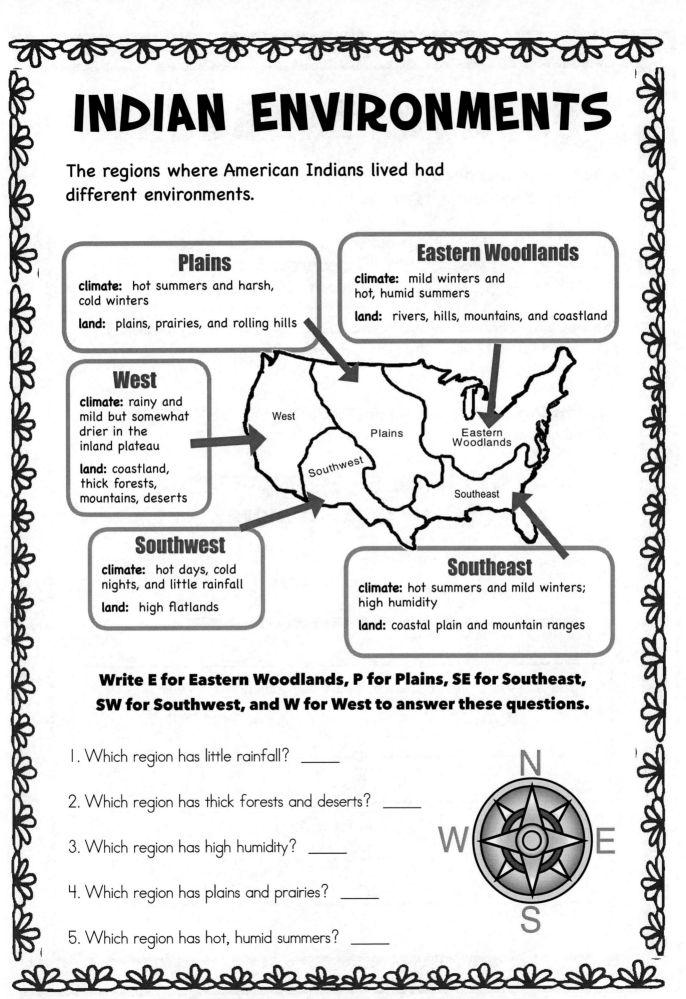

Plains
climate: hot summers and harsh, cold winters

land: plains, prairies, and rolling hills

Eastern Woodlands
climate: mild winters and hot, humid summers

land: rivers, hills, mountains, and coastland

West
climate: rainy and mild but somewhat drier in the inland plateau

land: coastland, thick forests, mountains, deserts

Southwest
climate: hot days, cold nights, and little rainfall

land: high flatlands

Southeast
climate: hot summers and mild winters; high humidity

land: coastal plain and mountain ranges

Write E for Eastern Woodlands, P for Plains, SE for Southeast, SW for Southwest, and W for West to answer these questions.

1. Which region has little rainfall? _____

2. Which region has thick forests and deserts? _____

3. Which region has high humidity? _____

4. Which region has plains and prairies? _____

5. Which region has hot, humid summers? _____

INDIAN CULTURES

American Indians developed different cultures because they lived in different environments of North America.

 **culture:** the beliefs, customs, and way of life of a group of people
environment: surroundings

The Iroquois, Cherokee, Lakota, Pueblo, and Nez Perce peoples developed different cultures because they lived in different environments in North America.

Ways the Iroquois, Cherokee, Lakota, Pueblo, and Nez Perce cultures differed included:

food   homes   transportation   jobs   arts   & more!

Fill in the blanks to complete the cause-and-effect diagram.

Cause

The Southwest, Plains, Eastern Woodlands, Southeast, and West regions had ___ ___ ___ ___ ___ ___ ___ ___ ___ environments.

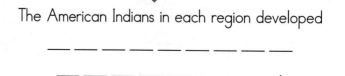

Effect

The American Indians in each region developed

___ ___ ___ ___ ___ ___ ___ ___ ___ ___

___ ___ ___ ___ ___ ___ ___ ___ ___ .

INDIANS USE THE ENVIRONMENT

American Indian tribes interacted with their environment. They used their **natural resources**. The natural resources available influenced how they met their needs.

Local natural resources include plants, animals, and materials that are available nearby.

The American Indians used their local natural resources to:
- build their homes
- make their clothes
- make their tools
- provide their food

Fill in the blanks with resources that people use today.

American Indians in the past

People in my community

1. deer meat and corn	← **Food** →	_____
2. stones and sticks	← **Tools** →	_____
3. animal hides	← **Clothes** →	_____
4. logs, bark, clay	← **Homes** →	_____

American Indian Homes

American Indians adapted to their environment in many different ways. One way was how they made their homes.

- The **Iroquois** lived in the Eastern Woodlands region. Many plants and trees grew here. The Iroquois lived in shelters made from bent poles, bark, and other plant materials.

- The **Lakota** lived in the Plains region. Many herds of buffalo roamed here. The Lakota lived in teepees made from buffalo hides.

- The **Cherokee** lived in the Southeast region. Using trees from nearby forests, the Cherokee built log houses and wood huts, as well as mud-covered lodges.

- The **Pueblo** lived in the Southwest region. This region was very dry, with few trees or animal herds. The Pueblo lived in adobe (clay), multi-terraced buildings.

- The **Nez Perce** lived in the West region. Most of the time, they lived in longhouses built from wood or sticks and covered with reeds, grasses, or skins. When they hunted, the Nez Perce lived in portable teepees.

Use the text to determine which American Indians lived in each home. Write Cherokee, Lakota, or Pueblo under each photograph.

_____   _____   _____

American Indian Clothing

American Indians used their environment to make clothes.

- The **Cherokee** Indians softened the skins of deer, bear, and beaver for their clothes.

- The **Iroquois** also made clothing, including shoes, from the hides (skin and fur) of the animals they hunted.

- The **Lakota** wore leather clothing made from deerskin, moccasins on their feet, and buffalo-hide robes in the winter.

- **Pueblo** clothing was made of animal skins and cotton, which they grew, or wool fiber.

- The **Nez Perce** used plant materials, hides, and fur to make their clothes.

**Why did many American Indians use animal skins for clothing?
Circle the correct answer or answers.**

Animal skins were warm.   **Many stores sold animal skins.**   **Many animals were available to hunt.**

Put a ✓ next to the statement that describes the main idea of this page.

_____ 1. American Indians made clothing from resources in their environment.

_____ 2. American Indians did not have to pay for their clothing.

_____ 3. American Indians traded their colorful clothing to other tribes.

_____ 4. American Indians wore different clothes than people do today.

What American Indians Ate

What American Indians ate depended on where they lived.

Many American Indians hunted for food. They hunted small animals like rabbits or larger animals like bears, deer, turkey, buffalo, elk, sea otters, or seals. They might use blowguns for smaller animals and bows and arrows for larger animals.

American Indians also fished, farmed, and gathered food. They used spears, traps, and hooks to catch fish and mussels. They grew crops like corn, squash, beans, and melons. They ate wild berries and nuts they found in the woods.

People today eat many of the same foods the American Indians ate.

Circle the picture that shows how people today get their food.

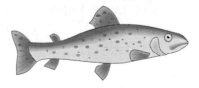

Circle the pictures that show foods the American Indians ate.

Underline the pictures that show foods we eat today.

AMERICAN INDIAN JOBS

The Iroquois, Cherokee, Lakota, Pueblo, and Nez Perce peoples had different jobs because they lived in different environments.

- The **Iroquois** were farmers, hunters, and gatherers. The season of the year determined how they found food.

- The **Cherokee** spent a lot of the year hunting deer to eat. They also gathered wild plants, fished, and grew vegetables.

- The **Lakota** were hunters and horsemen. They moved around the flat plains hunting for buffalo.

- The **Pueblo** were both farmers and hunters. The Southwest offered plenty of land, but the Pueblo had to grow crops that did not require much water.

- The **Nez Perce** got food from the thick forests where they lived. They hunted for big game like elk and moose. They also gathered various kinds of berries, plus roots to eat in winter.

You can make a chart!
Put a ✓ to show which occupations were common in each American Indian culture.

OCCUPATIONS

GROUPS	Fishermen	Hunters	Farmers	Horsemen
Iroquois				
Cherokee				
Lakota				
Pueblo				
Nez Perce				

American Indian Tools

American Indians used tools to survive. They made their tools by hand. They did not have electric tools like we do today.

Different Indian groups used different tools depending on their environment. American Indians used tools including:

- Axes to cut wood for homes, canoes, and other items
- Canoes and oars to travel on streams and rivers
- Blowguns, spears, and bows and arrows to hunt and protect themselves
- Snares, traps, and hooks to catch animals and fish
- Stone drills, hoes, and baskets to farm

Circle the American Indian tools in red.

Circle tools we use today in blue.

Match each tool to its use.

axe	travel on rivers
canoe	catch fish
bow/arrow	cut wood
fishing hook	hunt

American Indian Transportation

American Indians used different types of **transportation** because they lived in different regions of the United States.

- The **Iroquois** walked and paddled canoes made from trees. They used the canoes in lakes and rivers so they could fish for food.

- The **Lakota** moved around their region to hunt buffalo. At first they walked, pulling their belongings behind them. Later they used horses for transportation. Horses allowed them to travel fast across the flat plains. That was great for hunting buffalo!

- The **Pueblo** lived in villages. They walked to get around.

 **WORD TO KNOW!**

transportation: moving around

Answer the questions.

1. What features of the Eastern Woodlands led to the Iroquois' use of canoes?

_____

2. How and why did the Lakota move around before they began using horses?

_____

3. What activity allowed the Pueblo people to live in villages instead of moving from

place to place? _____

American Indian Contributions

American Indians have made and continue to make contributions to our present-day culture and how we live our lives today.

ARTS

- made pottery
- weaved thread into clothing
- carved wood into useful tools

weaving
pottery

KNOWLEDGE OF THE ENVIRONMENT

- taught each generation about the land and region

RESPECT FOR NATURE

- taught people to take care of nature: water, earth, air, animals, and plants

FARMING

- taught settlers how to farm
- taught settlers how to use available soil and water
- introduced crops like corn and tobacco

Tell why each American Indian contribution is important today.

ARTS

_____
_____
_____

KNOWLEDGE OF THE ENVIRONMENT

_____
_____
_____

RESPECT FOR NATURE

_____
_____
_____

FARMING

_____
_____
_____

American Indians Today

American Indian cultures have changed over time.

Today, many American Indian peoples still live in the same regions as their ancestors did. However, instead of living in towns, many American Indians live on reservations. A reservation is land set aside for American Indians by the U.S. government. Other American Indians live and work in cities and towns across America.

Wherever they live, many American Indians continue to practice their traditional cultures. They still create beautiful art. They still pass down knowledge of the environment and respect for nature to their children. They still use storytelling to keep their languages alive and pass down history and traditions!

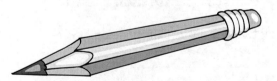

Write P if the statement was most likely said by an American Indian from the past.
Write T if the statement was most likely said by an American Indian today.

_____ 1. "I hunt wherever I want to. All the land around me belongs to my tribe."

_____ 2. "I live on a reservation with my family."

_____ 3. "I live in a teepee and ride a horse."

_____ 4. "I work in an office in a large city."

LEARN FROM BIOGRAPHIES

One person can change the world! It's true! Many people in America's past made the world a better place to live. These people include leaders, scientists, inventors, and explorers.

People who shaped today's world came from **diverse** backgrounds. But, they all made a difference!

A **biography** tells the story of a person's life. It describes important events in the person's life. You can use biographies to learn about people.

WORD TO KNOW! 👉 diverse: different; unalike

You can learn about:

- their character and beliefs
- when they lived
- what their life was like
- what they did
- where they lived
- how their actions made a difference

Use the Word Bank to complete each sentence.

People who make a difference in the world today come from diverse _____.
Their _____ helped shape our world today. You can learn about these people from _____.

Word Bank

actions
backgrounds
biographies

What information would a biography about you include?
Place a ✓ next to the correct answers.

_____ 1. When you were born   _____ 4. A picture of George Washington

_____ 2. Where you grew up   _____ 5. What you did in your life

_____ 3. How you changed the world _____ 6. A map of Alaska

Abraham Lincoln's Early Years

Abraham Lincoln was born in Kentucky in 1809. His family lived in a tiny log cabin on a small farm. When Abraham was young, his family moved to Indiana.

Abraham Lincoln's family did not have much money. Abraham often had to work to help his family. Because of that, he rarely was able to go to school.

Abraham Lincoln loved books and reading. He taught himself how to read, write, and do math. He walked for miles to borrow books and papers from people to read. Abraham even took a book with him when he plowed the fields!

Abraham Lincoln's cousin Dennis said this about Abraham:
"I never saw Abe after he was 12 that he didn't have a book in his hand or in his pocket."

**What does that quote tell you about Abraham Lincoln?
Circle the correct answer.**

He did not like farming.   His family was poor.   He loved to read.

**Write T for True and F for False.
Then correct any false statements to make them true.**

_____ 1. Abraham Lincoln was born in Kentucky.

_____ 2. Abraham Lincoln's family was poor.

_____ 3. Abraham Lincoln went to school every day.

_____ 4. Abraham Lincoln hated to read.

Abraham Lincoln, Hard Worker

Abraham Lincoln was a hard worker.

He had many different jobs. They included:
- shopkeeper – worked in a general store
- postmaster – delivered mail
- woodcutter – cut wood for fire
- surveyor – measured land
- soldier – served in the Black Hawk War

When he was about 25 years old, Abraham Lincoln was elected to the Illinois General Assembly. He decided to become a lawyer. At that time, law school was not required—you just had to pass a test to become a lawyer. Abraham passed the test.

Abraham Lincoln got a job with a law firm. He traveled around the state helping people with legal problems. People liked him. He explained things clearly to people, and he made them laugh!

Circle jobs Abraham Lincoln did during his young life.

ABRAHAM LINCOLN, PRESIDENT

Abraham Lincoln became more involved in government. He ran for more political offices. In 1860, he was elected the 16th President of the United States!

At that time in America, some states allowed slavery and some states did not. Most states in the South allowed slavery. States up North did not.

> The northern states were known as the "Union." The southern states were known as the "Confederacy."

Abraham Lincoln was against slavery. People in the South did not want him to be president. When Lincoln was elected, southern states started to leave the Union. They decided to form their own country!

President Lincoln said, "You cannot do that!"
Soon, the Civil War began between the North and the South.

This map shows the U.S. when the Civil War started in 1861. Follow the instructions.

1. Use a blue crayon to draw a circle around the northern states.

2. Use a red crayon to draw a circle around the southern states.

3. Find your state on the map. Circle it in green.

North

South

Free States and Territories
Undecided Territories
Slave States

Lincoln for Freedom!

President Lincoln wanted to free the slaves in the South. During the Civil War, he issued an important document. This document was called the **Emancipation Proclamation**. It stated that all enslaved people in the Confederate states should be free!

But there was a problem. The Confederate states ignored the proclamation. They did not recognize President Lincoln as their leader. But soon, the North won the Civil War, and slavery ended in the United States!

Abraham Lincoln was one of America's greatest presidents. He kept the United States together as one nation after a terrible war. He also passed laws that freed slaves!

 **WORDS TO KNOW!**

> **emancipation:** the freeing of someone from slavery
>
> **proclamation:** an important announcement

President Lincoln changed history! Read the actions. Then choose the effect of each action.

_____ 1. President Lincoln issued the Emancipation Proclamation.
    A. Slaves in the Confederate states were free.
    B. Slaves were paid money for their work.

_____ 2. The Union won the Civil War.
    A. The United States broke apart.
    B. The United States remained together.

_____ 3. The Union won the Civil War.
    A. Slavery continued in the South.
    B. Slaves were set free in America.

Martin Luther King Jr.'s Early Years

Martin Luther King Jr. grew up in the South. At that time in the South, African Americans did not have the same rights as white people. Martin's father openly showed his dislike for **segregation** and **prejudice**. He taught his son that no person, and no race, was better than any other.

> **prejudice:** dislike for or distrust of people because they are of a different race or religion
>
> **segregation:** to be separated from other races

Martin Luther King Jr. went to Booker T. Washington High School. It was the first black public high school in Atlanta. He was an excellent student. Martin entered college when he was only 15! He decided to become a **minister** like his father.

Put a ✓ by the things Martin Luther King Jr. grew up with.

____equal rights   ____segregation   ____religion

____family   ____slavery   ____prejudice   ____liberty

**Words that have almost the same meaning are called synonyms.
Circle the synonym for the word "minister."**

trust   pastor   doctor

DR. KING, PASTOR

Martin Luther King Jr. preached his first sermon at his father's church, with great success. He became a pastor there.

Martin Luther King Jr. went to two more colleges in Pennsylvania and Massachusetts. He earned a special degree called a "doctorate" degree.

Martin Luther King Jr. met Coretta Scott in Boston. They got married. Martin and Coretta moved to Montgomery, Alabama. There, Martin became a minister at Dexter Avenue Baptist Church. People now called him <u>Dr.</u> Martin Luther King Jr.

1. Trace the path Martin Luther King Jr. took to complete his education.

2. In which direction did Martin Luther King Jr. travel from his home in Georgia?

north   south   east   west

3. When he finished college, Martin Luther King Jr. moved to Alabama. Draw an arrow from Massachusetts to Alabama. Which direction is your arrow pointing?

north   south   east   west

MARTIN LUTHER KING JR., LEADER

Martin Luther King Jr. became a **civil rights leader**.

Dr. King did not want violent protests where people could get hurt. He urged people to protest in nonviolent ways like marches, boycotts, prayer vigils, and **sit-ins**.

sit-in: a protest where people sit in a place and refuse to leave

One famous example of a sit-in happened in 1960. Four African American students sat at a lunch counter in Greensboro, North Carolina. They refused to leave until they were served. Many more peaceful sit-ins followed. Another famous sit-in occurred at Rich's Department Store in Atlanta. Dr. King was arrested there and sent to jail.

Martin Luther King Jr. was arrested many times during his fight for civil rights. But he continued to lead nonviolent protests throughout the South.

Number the events 1-4 in the order that they happened.

_____ Martin Luther King Jr. entered college at the age of 15.

_____ Martin Luther King Jr. was arrested at a sit-in in Atlanta.

_____ Martin Luther King Jr. organized a bus boycott.

_____ Martin Luther King Jr. married Coretta Scott.

A Man with A Dream

Martin Luther King Jr. led a peaceful protest in 1963 in Washington, D.C. It was called the "March on Washington." More than 250,000 people came from all over the United States. They called for equal rights for all Americans. Dr. King gave a famous speech at the march. His "I Have a Dream" speech is one of the most famous speeches of all time!

Here is a part of Dr. King's speech at the March on Washington. Use the Word Bank to fill in the blanks.

"I have a _____ that my four little

children will one day live in a _____

where they will not be judged by the

_____ of their _____

but by the content of their character."

Word Bank

color
dream
skin
nation

Is this speech a primary source?   **yes   no**

The March on Washington was a success! In the next two years, Congress passed important civil rights laws. Many of the things that Dr. King and others had been fighting for were coming to pass!

Benjamin Franklin, Founding Father

Benjamin Franklin was born in Boston, Massachusetts, in 1706. He was the 15th of 17 children!

Benjamin Franklin went to school for two years. But at age 10, Ben had to quit school. His father could not afford to send him anymore. Ben went to work in his father's soap and candle shop. Then, he worked as an **apprentice** in his brother's print shop.

 **apprentice:** someone who works for an expert to learn a trade

Why did Ben work instead of attend school?
Put a ✓ by the correct answer.

- ☐ 1. Ben did not like school.
- ☐ 2. Ben's father could not afford school.
- ☐ 3. There were no schools in Ben's town.

Benjamin Franklin moved to Philadelphia, Pennsylvania. He worked for several printers. Then he opened his own print shop.

During Benjamin Franklin's life, books and newspapers were very important in America. That was how people got their news. Ben was an excellent writer. He bought a newspaper and wrote a book called *Poor Richard's Almanac*. This book of clever sayings made Ben popular! We still use some of his sayings today.

Franklin the Statesman

Benjamin Franklin became involved in government. Pennsylvania voters elected him as one of their leaders.

At that time, Great Britain ruled over the American colonies. Many Americans were unhappy with British rules. Benjamin Franklin believed America should declare its independence. He was very wise, and people listened to him.

The American colonies went to war with Britain. America won the war and became a free nation! Benjamin Franklin signed both the **Declaration of Independence** and the **U.S. Constitution**.

Benjamin Franklin is remembered as one of America's greatest **statesmen**. He was a "Founding Father" of the United States!

statesman: a person who shows great wisdom in guiding the affairs of a government

Put a ✓ next to the sentence that Ben Franklin might say.

☐ 1. "I want Great Britain to rule America."

☐ 2. "I want America to be free from Great Britain."

☐ 3. "I signed the Declaration of Independence."

Circle the words that describe Ben Franklin.

author   **statesman**   **doctor**   **inventor**

Susan B. Anthony's Early Years

Susan B. Anthony

Susan B. Anthony was born in 1820 in Adams, Massachusetts. Her father was a Quaker. He did not believe in games and toys, but he did believe in education.

Unlike most Americans at that time, Susan's father believed women should get as much education as they wanted. He added a classroom to his house and hired a teacher for the children.

Circle the things that were a part of Susan's life as a child.

teacher   education   games   toys   computers

Susan B. Anthony finished her schooling at age 16. Teaching was one of the few jobs a woman could have at that time. So, Susan became a teacher.

When Susan complained because she was paid less than a male teacher, she was fired. Women faced many obstacles in that time in history.

Write T for True and F for False.
Then correct any false statements to make them true.

_____ 1. Susan's father believed that women should be educated.

_____ 2. Susan's father loved for Susan to play with games and toys.

_____ 3. When Susan complained because she was paid less than a male teacher, she got a raise.

_____ 4. Women have more job choices today than in the past.

Fight for Women's Rights

In 1851, Susan B. Anthony met Elizabeth Cady Stanton. They became lifelong friends. They were partners in shaping the women's **suffrage** movement.

 suffrage: right to vote in political elections

Elizabeth Cady Stanton

Susan devoted herself to the women's rights movement. She traveled the country making speeches and organizing state and national conventions for women's rights. She published a newspaper called *The Revolution*, which demanded equal rights for women.

**Write I by the way Susan was <u>influenced</u> by her environment.
Write A by the way Susan <u>adapted</u> to her environment.**

_____ grew up among Quakers   _____ published a newspaper

Women were not allowed to own property or vote in the 1850s. Susan B. Anthony collected signatures for a petition to grant women these rights. In 1860, New York passed a law that allowed women to make contracts and be in charge of their own money. However, New York did not agree to let women vote. It ws not until after her death that Susan's efforts finally achieved that goal.

Although Susan B. Anthony was passionate about her beliefs, she respected authority. She used peaceful means like speeches, petitions, and her newpaper to help achieve her goals.

**List three things Susan B. Anthony did to help
women get more rights.**

1. _____

2. _____

3. _____

ROSA PARKS RIDES THE BUS

Rosa Parks lived in Montgomery, Alabama. She rode the bus to work. In Montgomery, seats at the front of every bus were reserved for white passengers. Black passengers were not allowed to sit in those seats.

On December 1, 1955, Rosa Parks got on a bus. She was tired after working all day. She sat in the black section in the back of the bus. Soon all the white seats were filled, and more white passengers were getting on the bus. The bus driver told Rosa and other black people to give up their seats.

At first, the other black passengers refused to move. The driver said he would call the police. The black people moved, but Rosa Parks said no. She thought it was unfair!

Which word best describes what the Montgomery buses did?

fair   unfair

Circle the correct answer to each question.

1. How did Rosa Parks travel to her job?

drove a car   rode a bus

2. Why Rosa Parks sit in the back of the bus?

she was black   she liked the back

3. The bus driver told Rosa Parks to give up her seat. What did she do?

refused to give up her seat   gave up her seat

Rosa Parks Takes a Stand

Rosa Parks was arrested for not giving up her seat on the bus. The police took her to jail.

Rosa Parks being fingerprinted

Black leaders wanted to end segregation on buses in Montgomery. After Rosa Parks was arrested, they decided to start a bus **boycott** in the city. Leaders thought the boycott would cause the bus companies to lose money. Maybe then they would end segregation on the buses!

boycott: to stop buying or using something as a form of protest

Civil rights leaders printed flyers and handed them out. The flyers asked people not to ride the buses. People listened! People got to work in other ways, like walking, riding bikes, or using carpools. The Montgomery bus boycott lasted for 381 days.

Martin Luther King Jr. was one of the leaders of the Montgomery bus boycott.

A year has 365 days in it. The bus boycott lasted for 381 days. How many days beyond a year did the boycott last?

_____

Write 1, 2 or 3 to number the events in the order they happened.

_____ Flyers were handed out asking people not to ride the buses.

_____ Rosa Parks was arrested.

_____ A bus boycott began in Montgomery, Alabama.

What Government Does

The purpose of government in the United States is to protect the rights of citizens.

How does our government do that?

- makes laws
- enforces laws
- decides if laws are fair and if they have been broken
- provides public services like fire and police protection
- provides leadership to citizens

 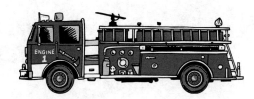 

Match each job of government to the example of it.

Government Roles

_____ 1. makes laws

_____ 2. provides leadership

_____ 3. provides public services

_____ 4. determines if laws have been broken

_____ 5. enforces laws

Examples

A. The mayor tells people what to do when a bad storm is coming.

B. Firemen help when buildings catch on fire.

C. The speed limit is set at 25 mph in a school zone.

D. The judge says, "You are guilty."

E. Police officers write tickets when people drive too fast.

Rules and Laws

Rules are guidelines for how people should act or behave. You probably have rules around the house, like "Clear your dishes off the table" or "Do not leave your shoes on the stairs." You also have rules in your classroom, like "Keep your hands to yourself," or "Raise your hand when you want to speak."

Laws are rules made by the government. Laws are very important in the daily life of a community. They provide important **benefits**.

Citizens are expected to follow the rules and laws of their home, school, and community. Here are some things rules and laws do:

- **Protect people's rights**
- **Keep order**
- **Keep people safe and secure**
- **Protect people's property**

Decide if each item is a rule or law.
Put a ✓ in the correct column of the chart.

Expectation	Rule	Law
1. Obey the speed limit.		
2. Raise your hand in class when you want to speak.		
3. Do your homework before you go out to play.		
4. Do not steal from stores.		
5. Stop at stop signs.		
6. Do not bring toys to the dinner table.		

Rules and Laws Create Order

Why do we have rules and laws? Rules and laws help:

create order   protect property   keep people safe

Rules and laws help people know how to act.
They tell people what they should and should not do.
People must follow the rules—or face the consequences.

Match the beginning of each sentence to the best ending.

_____ 1. If you get to work late every day,

_____ 2. If you do not listen while the teacher is talking,

_____ 3. If you do not do your homework,

_____ 4. If you do not follow safety rules,

A. you will not learn the lesson.

B. you might get hurt.

C. you might have to work on it during recess.

D. you might get fired from your job.

There are different rules for different places. Why? Because the way people should act is different depending on where they are. Also, some rules only make sense for certain places.

Match each rule to where it makes sense.

_____ 1. Make up your bed.

_____ 2. Raise your hand to speak.

_____ 3. Don't speed.

_____ 4. Share the kickball.

_____ 5. Read quietly.

A. playground

B. highway

C. library

D. home

E. school

DIFFERENT RULES FOR DIFFERENT PLACES

There are different rules for behavior in different places.

Name the place where each rule applies.

- ➡ Write HO for home.
- ➡ Write CO for community.
- ➡ Write HW for highway.

- ➡ Write CL for classroom.
- ➡ Write PL for playground.

_____ 1. Raise your hand before asking a question.

_____ 2. Help clear the table after eating a meal.

_____ 3. Do not litter the park.

_____ 4. Take turns choosing what game to play.

_____ 5. Obey the traffic signals to cross the street.

_____ 6. Do not throw a ball at a student's head.

_____ 7. Straighten up your room before going outside to play.

_____ 8. Write your name at the top corner of your test.

_____ 9. Feed the dog every day.

_____ 10. Do not go beyond the fence or into the street.

_____ 11. Follow all the rules of the road when driving.

_____ 12. Do not go in someone else's home without permission.

Predict how people would act if there were no rules at school.

_____

_____

_____

Government Leaders

There are leaders in your city.
There are leaders in your state.
There are leaders in your country, too!

- The leader of a city is the mayor.
- The leader of the state is the governor.
- The leader of the nation is the president.

American citizens can vote in elections!
Voters in the United States elect government leaders to make decisions for them in the national government.
This means that every leader is chosen by the people!

Match each statement with a leader who might make it.

_____ 1. "I am proud to lead the United States of America."

_____ 2. "I am going to make some changes in this city."

_____ 3. "This state has a lot to be proud of."

A. mayor

B. governor

C. president

You can vote in your classroom to make classroom decisions.
Work in small groups. Think of two new rules for your classroom.
Write your rules here.

Rule #1 _____

Rule #2 _____

Compare your rules with other groups' rules.
Did any groups make the same rules? _____
Vote to choose the rules people want.

CAPITAL CITIES

A **capital** is the city where official government business takes place.

The leader of our <u>country</u> works in the U.S. capital city. **Washington, D.C.** is the capital of the United States.

Draw a red circle around the star for Washington, D.C.

Washington, D.C.

The leader of our <u>state</u> works in the state capital city.

Put a star on the map in the location of your state's capital. Label the star with the name of the capital city.

Circle the correct answer.

Our state capital is _____ of Washington, D.C.

north	**northeast**
south	**southwest**
east	**northwest**
west	**southeast**

Where Leaders Work

White House

The president of the United States works in Washington, D.C., the nation's capital. The president works in the **White House**, and he or she lives there, too! The president has an office in the White House called the Oval Office.

The governor of our state works in the **State Capitol Building**. Many state capitol buildings are beautiful places that citizens love to visit!

A State Capitol

A City Hall

The mayor of a city works in that city. The mayor works in a building known as **City Hall**. City halls are many different sizes, depending on the size of the city.

Match each leader to where he or she works.

President of the United States   **City Hall**

Governor of our state   **State Capitol Building**

Mayor   **White House**

What Good Citizens Do

Citizens have **responsibilities**.

A responsibility is something you are expected to do.

For example:
- Your parents might expect you to make your bed every day.
- Your teacher might expect you to do your homework every day.

A responsibility is also a way you are expected to act.

For example:
- Your parents might expect you to treat other children nicely on the playground.
- Your teacher expects you to wait your turn or help another student who drops a book.

Practice these responsibilities to be a good citizen:

1. respect and protect the rights and property of others
2. vote to make classroom decisions
3. take actions to improve the school and community
4. show self-discipline and self-reliance
5. be honest and trustworthy
6. know the purposes of rules and laws, and obey them

 citizen: a person who is part of a community

Circle the things a good citizen would do.

GOOD CITIZENS RESPECT & PROTECT!

Good citizens **respect** and **protect** the rights and property of others.

You can show respect by being kind and courteous to other people. You can show respect by being fair. You can show respect by listening when other people talk.

You can protect the property of others by taking care of other people's things. For example, if you borrow a book from your friend, you keep it safe until you give it back to him or her. In the classroom, you can take care of things that everyone shares, like books, toys, and markers.

Read Joe's story.

Joe borrowed his friend's truck so he could work on his yard.
He used the truck all weekend to haul dirt, plants, and tools.
Joe needs to return the truck this afternoon, but it is a mess!
The truck is covered in dirt inside and out!
The gas tank is empty, too.

Circle the pictures that show what Joe should do to show respect to his friend.

Using good manners is another great way to show respect. Add words to the conversation that help show respect for others.

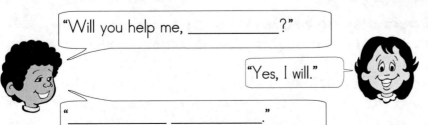

"Will you help me, _____?"

"Yes, I will."

" _____."

It is easy to know how to treat others with respect:

Treat other people as you want them to treat you!

Good Citizens Are Accountable

You are **accountable** for your personal actions.
Personal actions are the things you do and say. You choose how to act every day.

When you choose to do things that are good, healthy, or right, you **make responsible choices**. For example, putting your toys away when you are done playing is a responsible choice.

 **accountable:** responsible for your own choices and actions

Choose the responsible choice for each situation.

It is 10 p.m. on a school night. What would you do?

☐ stay up later
☐ go to bed

What do you choose for your after-school snack?

☐ banana
☐ candy

Should you brush your teeth before bed?

☐ Yes
☐ No

When you choose to be responsible for your actions, you **take responsibility**. If you make a mess, you should clean it up. If you break something, you should try to fix it. If you hurt someone's feelings, you should try to make him or her feel better.

Imagine you were playing ball inside and you broke a lamp. Circle the comments that show being accountable.

I'm sorry.   It is not my fault.   I will pay for it.

I made a mistake.   I do not know who did it.

GOOD CITIZENS VOTE!

A good citizen votes! When you **vote**, you help decide how things should be done. Voting in the classroom is important because it gives everyone an equal chance to make important decisions. Your opinion matters!

One way to participate in decision-making in your classroom is by voting on class rules.

Look at the two lists of rules below. Circle your vote under each list.

A
Classroom Rules

1. Talk whenever and however loudly you want.
2. Don't do your homework.
3. Don't listen.
4. Don't be on time.

My Vote: YES   NO

B
Classroom Rules

1. Do not talk when the teacher is talking.
2. Do your homework.
3. Listen to others.
4. Be on time.

My Vote: YES   NO

Why are classroom decisions important?
Match each rule with the reason for it.

_____ 1. Do not talk when the teacher is talking.

_____ 2. Do your homework.

_____ 3. Listen to others.

_____ 4. Keep your area neat.

A. It will support what you learned in class.

B. The classroom needs to be organized.

C. You need to hear important things being said.

D. You need to show respect for others.

Good Citizens Improve

Good citizens try to **improve** the world around them. One way you can do that is by doing things to help your school and your community. Good citizens see things that need to be done and take action!

For example, you might see a spot outside your school with a lot of weeds in it. You could ask some friends to help you pull the weeds to make the area look nicer. In your community, you might want to help pick up trash at the local park.

Which statements describe actions that could improve your school? Write YES next to actions that would improve it. Write NO next to actions that would not improve it.

_____ 1. Let's have a food fight in the cafeteria!

_____ 2. Let's pick up trash around our school.

_____ 3. Let's add a bin for recyclable cans in the cafeteria.

_____ 4. Let's splash water on the floor in the bathroom.

Which statements describe actions that could improve your community? Write YES next to actions that would improve it. Write NO next to actions that would not improve it.

_____ 1. Let's visit the elderly at the retirement home.

_____ 2. Let's collect toys to give to needy children.

_____ 3. Let's run through the aisles at the grocery store.

_____ 4. Let's volunteer to paint the mailboxes on our street.

Self-Discipline and Self-Reliance

Good citizens demonstrate self-discipline and self-reliance.

Self-discipline is controlling your actions all by yourself. You use self-discipline to stay quiet when the teacher is talking or when you share toys with a friend.

Self-reliance is being independent. When you are self-reliant, you can do things on your own.
Self-reliant people take care of themselves.
They do their chores without being asked to do them.
They get dressed or brush their teeth without help.

Decide if the actions below show self-discipline or self-reliance.
Write SD by the ones that show <u>self-discipline</u>.
Write SR by the ones that show <u>self-reliance</u>.

_____ 1. brushing my teeth each day

_____ 2. keeping my hands to myself in the classroom

_____ 3. getting up when my alarm rings

_____ 4. sharing toys with my friend

_____ 5. putting away my clothes in my room

_____ 6. staying quiet when the teacher is talking

_____ 7. making my bed each day

_____ 8. not interrupting adults when they are talking

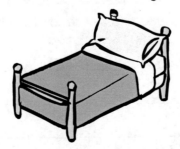

Good Citizens are Honest and Trustworthy!

Good citizens are **honest**. Being honest means you do not lie. Being honest means:
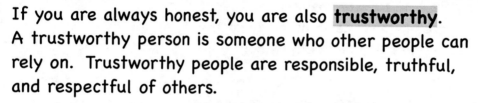
- You tell the truth.
- You do not hide the truth to avoid trouble.
- You do not cheat or steal.

If you are always honest, you are also **trustworthy**. A trustworthy person is someone who other people can rely on. Trustworthy people are responsible, truthful, and respectful of others.

Circle the correct answers.

An honest person:

admits that they broke their mom's mirror	**YES**	**NO**
copies homework from a friend	**YES**	**NO**
admits to starting the fight with their sister	**YES**	**NO**

A trustworthy person:

keeps a secret a friend has told them	**YES**	**NO**
tells stories about others	**YES**	**NO**
cleans their room when their dad asks them to	**YES**	**NO**

Read the story. Answer the questions.

You are only allowed to play video games for 30 minutes at night. Your mom said to stop when the buzzer sounded and get ready for bed. When you heard the buzzer ring, you didn't stop playing.

Was that an honest thing to do? _____

Why? _____

_____

United We Stand!

People in America have many differences. However, we are united as American citizens!

The basic principles of our **republican form of government** bring us together. These basic principles include the individual rights to:

Life: the right to live safe from harm

Liberty: the right to freedom

Pursuit of happiness: the right to do what makes you happy

Equality under the law: fair and equal treatment

A republican form of government allows the people to elect their leaders. Those leaders make the laws for everyone.

Circle the individual right each quotation describes.

1. "I want to be a doctor when I grow up."

pursuit of happiness   **life**

2. "I am treated the same as every other American citizen."

equality under the law   **pursuit of happiness**

3. "I can speak out about a law I don't like in America."

pursuit of happiness   **liberty**

We Are a Team

People often work together as part of a group.
Some of the reasons people work together in groups include:

- to complete tasks
- to achieve goals
- to solve problems

 **group:** two or more people connected by a place, activity, or purpose

Goals can often be accomplished better and faster by a group than by people working on their own.

Circle the things that a group could accomplish better or faster than an individual person.

build a storage shed for playground equipment

pick up litter around your school

plant a garden

make a phone call

Groups usually form for a purpose or goal. That purpose could be to complete a class project, to play a game, to help the community, or anything else.

Match the group of people working together to what they want to achieve.

_____ 1. children in a classroom

_____ 2. people at a business

_____ 3. people on a sports team

_____ 4. people in a town or city

A. to solve a community problem

B. to finish a job quickly

C. to understand a lesson

D. to win a game

Let's Cooperate

A group is made up of different people. Sometimes, people have different ideas about how to do things. To be successful, everyone in the group needs to **cooperate**.

cooperate: work together to get something done

People can cooperate by using personal skills. **Personal skills** include:

- managing conflicts in a peaceful way, *like taking turns or voting*
- showing courtesy to others, *like speaking kindly, or following rules*
- respecting others, *like listening carefully and quietly*
- using self-control, *like not shouting or crying when upset*

Put a ✓ next to the statements that show cooperation.

_____ 1. "I am going to do it the way I want."

_____ 2. "That is a good idea. We can try doing it that way."

_____ 3. "She never does anything right."

_____ 4. "I do not want him in our group."

_____ 5. "Tell me what you think."

Suggest how personal skills could be used to help each group cooperate.

1. The reading group disagrees about what book to read.

_____

2. Two students in computer club want to use the same computer at the same time.

_____

3. People in the class keep shouting out their ideas for the book fair.

_____

American Symbols

The United States has many **patriotic symbols**!

American Flag

The United States has a national flag.

We call it the **American flag**. The American flag is an important symbol. It represents the United States.

When we see it flying high, it makes us proud to be Americans!

> The American flag has 50 stars. There is one star for each state. The flag has 13 stripes. They represent the original 13 colonies that declared independence from Great Britain!

Answer the questions.

1. The American flag symbolizes _____

2. How many stars are on the American flag? _____

3. The stars on the flag symbolize _____.

4. The stripes symbolize the 13 _____ that declared independence from Great Britain!

Bald Eagle

Another symbol of the United States is the **bald eagle**. The bald eagle is America's national bird. It was chosen because of its strength, long life, and dignified appearance. The bald eagle is not bald! It has a brown body with a white head.

Circle the words that describe the bald eagle.

long life   **weak**   **dignified**   **white head**   **strong**

PATRIOTIC MONUMENTS

American symbols include structures known as **monuments**.

 **WORD TO KNOW!** **monument:** something built to remember people or events

WASHINGTON MONUMENT

The Washington Monument is located in Washington, D.C. It was built to honor George Washington, America's first president. The Washington Monument is more than 500 feet tall. Fifty flags surround the base of the monument. They represent the 50 states in the United States.

STATUE OF LIBERTY

The Statue of Liberty is located in New York City. The country of France gave the huge copper statue to the United States in 1886. It was given as a sign of friendship. The Statue of Liberty symbolizes freedom!

> The Statue of Liberty sits on Liberty Island in New York Harbor. When immigrants came to America on ships in the 1800s and early 1900s, the statue greeted them.
> It became a worldwide symbol of freedom and democracy!

Decide which monument is being described in each statement.
Write WM for Washington Monument.
Write SL for Statue of Liberty.

_____ 1. located in New York City

_____ 2. located in Washington, D.C.

_____ 3. honors America's first president

_____ 4. symbol of freedom around the world

_____ 5. gift from France

_____ 6. surrounded by 50 flags

_____ 7. is located on an island

_____ 8. made of copper

PLEDGE OF ALLEGIANCE

America has many patriotic **traditions**!

 **tradition:** a belief or custom handed down from one generation to another

PLEDGE OF ALLEGIANCE

One of our patriotic traditions is saying the Pledge of Allegiance. American citizens say the Pledge of Allegiance to show respect for the American flag and for the United States.

Say the Pledge of Allegiance aloud. Put your right hand over your heart and stand at attention. Be respectful when you say it.

When you pledge allegiance to your country, you promise to be loyal to America!

> I pledge allegiance
> To the flag
> Of the United States
> of America
> And to the republic for which
> it stands,
> One nation under God,
> Indivisible,
> With liberty and
> justice for all.

In the text of the Pledge of Allegiance above, circle each word listed below. Then find the definitions of the words in a dictionary. Match each word to its definition.

_____ 1. pledge   A. freedom

_____ 2. allegiance   B. loyalty

_____ 3. republic   C. fairness

_____ 4. indivisible   D. to promise

_____ 5. liberty   E. unable to be divided

_____ 6. justice   F. form of government where people elect their leader

HONOR OUR SOLDIERS

U.S. citizens celebrate American **holidays**.
Many of our holidays recognize and honor events
and people who made our country great. Americans
demonstrate good citizenship when we celebrate holidays.

Americans celebrate two holidays each year to honor
men and women who have served our country in the military.
These brave soldiers have made great sacrifices to protect
our freedom!

Veterans Day is observed in November.
Veterans Day is a day to recognize and show respect for Americans who
served in the military. It is a day to remember their patriotism and
willingness to protect the United States.

Memorial Day is observed in May.
Memorial Day is a day to recognize and show respect for
Americans who died in wars while serving their country.
This day of remembrance started after the Civil War.
Its original name was "Decoration Day"—a day to decorate
the graves of soldiers.

Answer the questions.

1. In what month do we observe Memorial Day? _____

2. In what month do we observe Veterans Day? _____

3. What is similar about Memorial Day and Veterans Day?

_____

_____

4. What is the difference between Memorial Day and Veterans Day?

_____

_____

Honor Great Americans

Americans celebrate holidays to remember people who have made important contributions to America! For example:

Columbus Day is observed in October.
This is a day to remember Christopher Columbus. He was an Italian explorer. Christopher Columbus led the way for European exploration and colonization of the Americas!

Presidents' Day is observed in February.
This is a day when we honor all presidents of the United States, especially George Washington. George Washington was the first U.S. president.

Martin Luther King Jr. Day is observed in January.
This is a day to remember Martin Luther King Jr. He was an African American minister who worked so all people would be treated fairly. Martin Luther King Jr. changed America!

Complete the chart.

Holiday	Who is Honored	When Observed
Columbus Day		
Presidents' Day		
Martin Luther King Jr. Day		

Honor Important Events

Some American holidays celebrate important events and achievements in our country's history!

Independence Day (Fourth of July) is observed on July 4th. This is a day to remember when the United States became a new country. It is sometimes called "America's birthday!" The Fourth of July celebrates our freedom! People love to celebrate this holiday with fireworks, parades, and cookouts!

Thanksgiving Day is observed in November. This is a day to remember when the Pilgrims shared their harvest with the American Indians to say thank you for helping them survive. At Thanksgiving, we give thanks for the good things in our lives!

Labor Day is observed in September. This is a day dedicated to appreciating the contributions of the working class in America. Working people build our country's strength every day. Their hard work and achievements make America great!

Circle the holiday that fits each description.

1. Celebrates achievements of American workers

   Independence Day   **Thanksgiving Day**   **Labor Day**

2. Celebrates when America became a new country

   Independence Day   **Thanksgiving Day**   **Labor Day**

3. Celebrates when Pilgrims and American Indians shared their food

   Independence Day   **Thanksgiving Day**   **Labor Day**

GOODS AND SERVICES

Goods are objects that can satisfy people's wants. Goods can be touched or held. Examples of goods are products like homes, cars, furniture, food, and clothing.

Services are actions that can satisfy people's wants. Services cannot be touched or held. Examples of services are teaching a class, giving a haircut, babysitting, and repairing a car.

Write G under each good. Write S under each service.

_____ _____ _____ _____ _____

Describe a service each of these people provides.

Doctor

_____
_____
_____

Waitress

_____
_____
_____

Principal

_____
_____
_____

Airline pilot

_____
_____
_____

Economic Choices

People want many things. Our wants are **unlimited**.

Resources are things used to meet our wants. A resource can be materials, money, people, or equipment. Resources are **limited**.

Since limited resources cannot meet unlimited wants, people have to make choices. People cannot have everything they want!

The inability to meet all wants because of limited resources is called **scarcity**. Scarcity causes people to have to make choices.

Read each story. Help each person make a good choice.

1. Jane's grandmother gave her $20 for her birthday.

   Her old backpack has big holes in it. Jane went shopping for a new backpack.

   At the store, she saw a stuffed dog. It was so cute!

   Jane has to make a choice:

   ___ a) She should buy the backpack.

   ___ b) She should buy the stuffed dog.

2. Joey needs new tires for his car, because they are worn down and might go

   flat. He has just enough money to pay for new tires. Joey also wants to go to a

   soccer game. Decisions, decisions! Should Joey:

   ___ a) use his money to buy a ticket to the soccer game?

   ___ b) get new tires for his car and watch the game on TV?

ECONOMIC CHOICES

Resources are **limited**.

Producers and consumers must decide how to use resources. They must make economic choices.

When people choose one thing, they give up something else.

Complete this chart by making economic choices as a <u>producer</u>:

Limited Resources	Choices for producer	What would you <u>choose</u>?
Materials	Sell lemonade or fruit punch	
Kitchen space	Sell pizza or hamburgers	
Time	Be a teacher or a doctor	
Money	Buy cookies to sell or save money	

Complete this chart by making economic choices as a <u>consumer</u>:

Limited Resources	Choices for consumer	What would you <u>give up</u>?
Money	Buy toy or save money	
Time	Go to movie or go skating	
Tokens	Play game or get candy	
Space	Get bunk beds or canopy bed	

OPPORTUNITY COST

When you make a choice, you get something and you give up something. The thing you choose is what you get. The thing you do not choose is what you give up. What you give up is your **opportunity cost**.

You only have one dollar so you have to choose between a toy or candy.

Circle your choice.

Draw a square around your opportunity cost.

For each row in the chart, circle your choice in the center column. Then write the opportunity cost in the last column.

Limited Resources	Choices for Consumers	Opportunity Cost
Money	Go to a ball game or have a pizza	
Time	Go to a movie or go skating	
Tokens	Play game or get candy	
Space	Get bunk beds or a king-sized bed	

Costs and Benefits

A **benefit** is a way something is good for you.
A **cost** is what you give up for something.

If you decide to save your allowance for a month you could have a lot of money. That is the benefit of saving. The cost of saving was the candy or toy you gave up for a month to save all the money!

You have five dollars. You decide to save the five dollars instead of buying a scooter.

**Circle your benefit.
Draw a square around
your cost.**

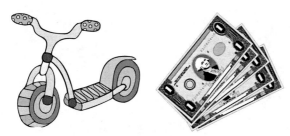

Your friend also has five dollars. Your friend decides to buy a scooter with the five dollars.

**Circle your friend's benefit.
Draw a square around your
friend's cost.**

Your dad has $500. He decides to save the money instead of buying a new computer.

**Circle your dad's benefit.
Draw a square around his cost.**

What is a future benefit of saving money? _____

_____

Use My Resource!

Resources can be used in a variety of ways.

Choose a resource. Examples might be things that come from nature, like water, oil, or trees. Write the name of the resource in the center of the graphic organizer. In the circles, draw or write several ways your resource can be used. You can add more circles if you have even more ideas.

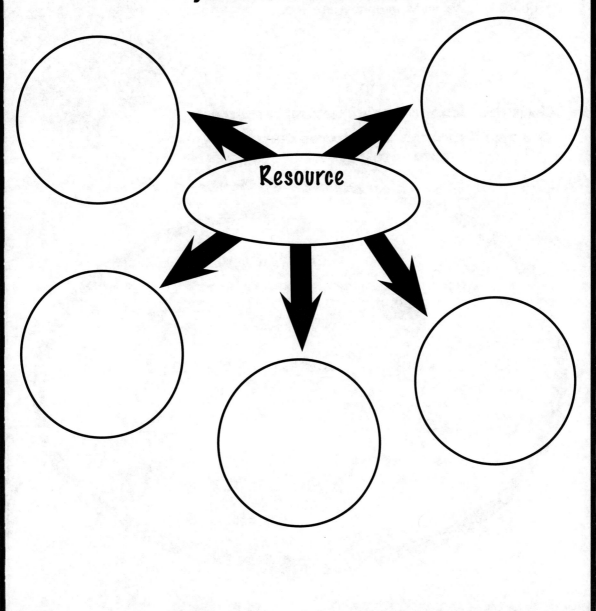

Resource

NATURAL RESOURCES

Natural resources are materials that come directly from nature. Examples of natural resources are water, soil, wood, and coal.

- Natural resources can be used by people to meet their wants.

- Natural resources can be used to produce goods and services people want, too.

Circle the pictures that are natural resources.

Draw an X through the pictures that are not natural resources.

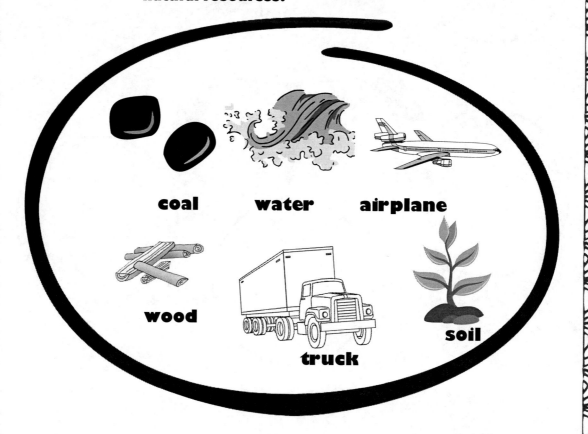

coal water airplane

wood truck soil

HUMAN RESOURCES

Human resources are people working to produce goods and services. Examples of human resources are farmers, miners, builders, and painters.

Human resources include people and their skills, talents, and knowledge.

Match each human resource to the good or service he or she provides.

CAPITAL RESOURCES

Capital resources are goods that are used to produce other goods and services.
Capital resources are the tools and equipment people use to do their jobs.

Examples of capital resources are hammers, computers, trucks, lawn mowers, and buildings.

Each person below needs a capital resource to do his or her job. Choose the right capital resource from the Word Bank. Write the correct word in each blank.

Word Bank

hammer   truck   building
computer   lawn mower

Human Resource	Capital Resource	How Human Resource Uses Capital Resource
truck driver	✚	The truck driver can deliver food to grocery stores.
builder	✚	The builder can connect boards to build a house.
landscaper	✚	The landscaper can mow the grass.
scientist	✚	The scientist can look up information.
factory worker	✚	The factory worker can work here to build cars.

ALLOCATION

Who gets goods and services? There are many different ways to **allocate**, or decide who gets them. These methods include:

Price is one way to allocate goods and services.
If the price is low, many people can buy the good or service.
If the price is high, few people can buy it.

Match each price with the number of people likely to pay it.

$5.00

$100.00

Another way to allocate goods and services is **majority rule**.
In this method, people vote to decide. Then goods and services are allocated based on how most of the people voted.

Circle the picture that shows majority rule.

Other ways to allocate goods and services include **sharing, using force, holding contests** or **lotteries**, and **first come/first served**.

ADVANTAGES OF MONEY

Money is called a **medium of exchange**. That means you can trade money for what you need or want.

Money makes it easy to buy goods and services. Money has a set value. Money is easy to carry with you.

When you go to the store, you can see the price of what you want and trade that amount of money for it!

 money: coins, paper bills, and checks used in exchange for goods and services

Write T for True or F for False.
Then correct any false statements to make them true.

_____ People work at jobs to earn money.

_____ Money cannot be used to buy services.

_____ Money is a medium of exchange.

_____ Money can buy goods.

These are things you could trade to get goods and services.
Write M for the ones that are money.

I'LL TRADE YOU FOR IT

Long ago, before there was money, people traded with each other. They exchanged goods and services with other people for what they needed. This kind of trade is called barter. People got goods and services through bartering.

Farmers and craftspeople could not use everything they grew or made. And they could not grow or make everything they needed. So, they bartered some of what they had for other things they needed.

Which is an example of bartering?
Write your answer here. _____

1. paying money for a candy bar

2. using a credit card to buy shoes

3. exchanging a bag of pretzels for some cookies

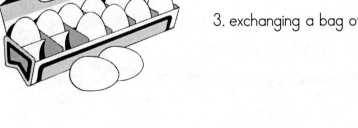

What if you had to barter for everything you needed?
How might you get a new pair of shoes?

_____

_____

Work Earns Money

People make money, or earn **income**, by working at jobs. People use their skills and training to do their jobs. Some examples of jobs include working as a teacher, a doctor, or a construction worker.

WORD TO KNOW!

income: money received, on a regular basis, for work

People spend the money they earn to buy the things they need and want.

Some things people spend money on are food, clothing, and a home to live in. People also spend money on things they want but don't need. For example, your dad may want to buy tickets to a baseball game. He does not need to go to the game but he wants to go. He will use the money he earns from his job to pay for the tickets.

Circle the correct ending to make this sentence true.

People earn income by _____.

saving money   spending money

working at a job

Put a ✓ under the pictures that show ways to earn money.

Why Save Money?

People can spend the money they earn or they can **save** it. When people save money, that money adds up over time. Money saved can be used to buy goods and services in the future.

People can use saved money to buy goods and services they need, like getting a car repaired. People also can use saved money to buy goods and services they want, like going on a vacation.

Read the stories and answer the questions.

Rachel and Evan each gets a $10 weekly allowance for doing chores at home.

Evan likes to play video games. He wants to buy a new game that costs $50 but he doesn't have $50. Every week, he spends his allowance on candy, ice cream, and little toys at the dollar store.

Rachel likes to draw and color. She wants to buy a new art set that costs $50. She decides to save her allowance to buy the art set. After five weeks, she has enough money to buy the art set.

1. Who spent money every week? _____

2. Who saved money every week? _____

3. What was Evan's opportunity cost? _____

4. What was Rachel's opportunity cost? _____

Producers and Consumers

People are buyers of goods and services. Another name for buyers is **consumers**. Consumers use goods and services.

People also use resources to make goods and provide services. When they do, they are called **producers**.

People are both consumers and producers of goods and services in their community. For example, Clara the hair stylist provides a service when she cuts your hair. She is a producer when she is at work. When Clara buys groceries after work, she is a consumer.

**Each photograph shows a producer and a consumer.
Write P next to each person acting as a producer.
Write C next to each person acting as a consumer.**

Two Sides

Sequence of Events

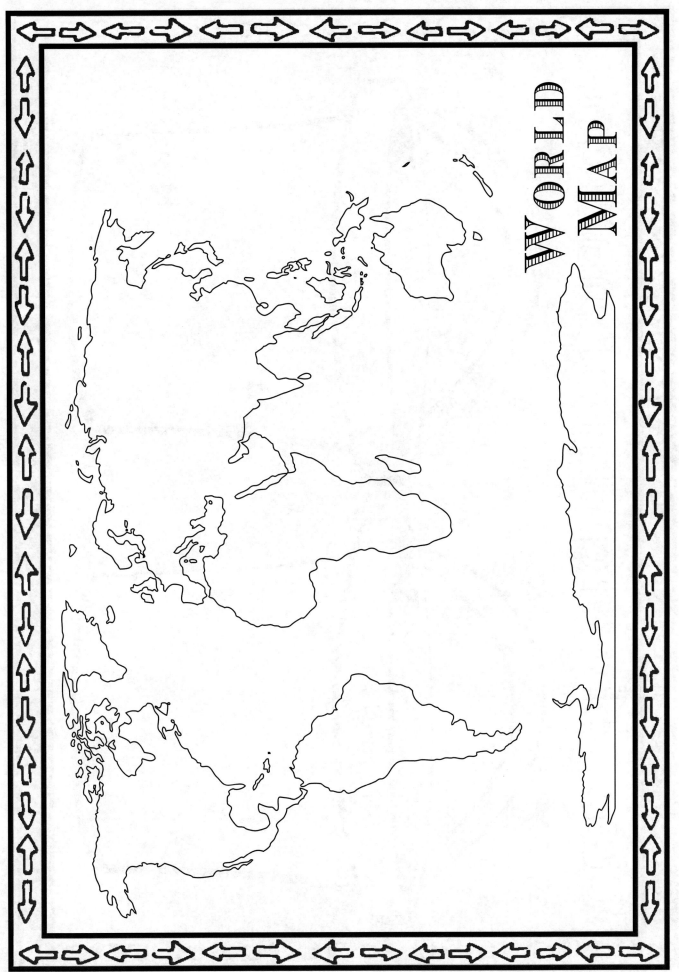

WORLD MAP

Classifying Information

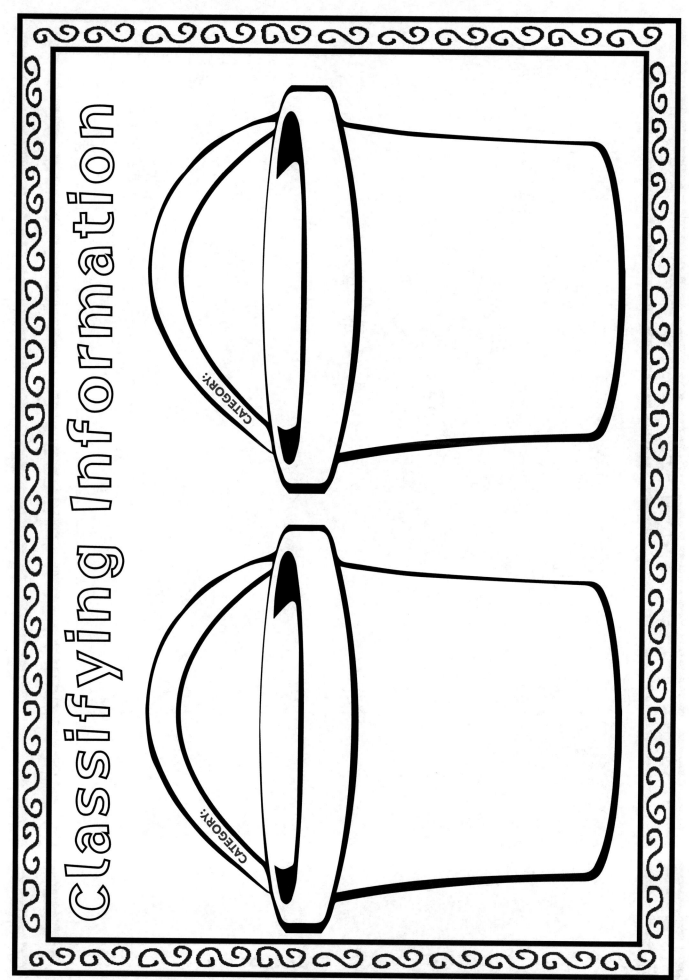

CATEGORY:

CATEGORY:

Wheel Diagram

Writing Prompts

HUMAN CHARACTERISTICS BRING CHANGE

Human characteristics are things people have added to a place and ways that people have changed the environment. List several such changes you have noticed that were recently added to your neighborhood or community. Possible examples are new houses or businesses, or new or expanded roads. Next to each human characteristic, explain how you think it will improve your community.

The Life of an American Indian

Imagine you are an American Indian living in your state 300 years ago. What do you eat? Where do you sleep? How do you stay warm? What do you wear? To answer these and other questions, think about the environment and natural resources available then. Next, come up with ways to meet your needs. Brainstorm answers to these questions and write them down.

THE LIFE OF A COLONIST

Think about all the ways life was more difficult for someone your age during a family's first year in a new colony in North America. Food and water were harder to get. Shelter was less comfortable. The family needed more work from the children. Everyone had to worry about whether local American Indians were friendly. Keeping all those things in mind, write a journal or diary entry about a day in the life of that child.

Writing Prompts

Your Autobiography

Write a short autobiography of your life so far. Start by making a list of important events (birth year, year you started school, years you moved, etc.). Then, write about important events in your life. Be sure to use full sentences and words that show chronological order, like "first," "In 2011," "before," "then," etc.

Changing Your World

Explain one way in which you would like to change the world or your community. Your goal does not need to be as major as Abraham Lincoln's desire to free slaves! You can make a big difference by volunteering or leading a community project, for example.

All About Benjamin Franklin

Write a short biography about the life of Benjamin Franklin. Then brainstorm about a fun field trip to learn more about Benjamin Franklin or his inventions. Suggest that field trip right after the biography.

Writing Prompts

Why Rules Matter

Pretend a new student has joined your class.
He or she does not know any of the class rules for proper behavior, using technology at school, and so on.
Write a short letter to him or her listing several school rules and explaining why these rules should be followed.

Make Good Choices

Think about all the choices you made yesterday. For example, you might have chosen to play a video game after school, or you might have chosen to play outside with your friends. You might have chosen between chips or fruit for a snack. Write at least four choices you made. Describe the benefit of each choice. Then describe your opportunity cost.

Identify Resources

One type of resource is people, like teachers in a school or nurses at the hospital. These are **human resources**. List as many human resources as you can. Another type of resource comes from nature, like trees or soil. These are **natural resources**. List as many natural resources as you can. A third type of resource can be equipment, like machines in a factory or pencils in a classroom. These are capital resources. List as many **capital resources** as you can.

Emphasize the Importance of Reading and Writing

Ask students to think of various things they can accomplish by reading and writing. Have each student create three "talking leaves" from construction paper. On each leaf, they will write something he or she can do by reading or writing. Examples might be, "I can write a letter to my grandmother," or "I can a read to my little brother." When everyone is finished, compare the talking leaves and tape them to the wall.

Learn to Use Social Studies Resources

Ask your students to think about where they would turn to find resources and tools that would help in social studies. Even in the digital age, hopefully they are thinking about reference books. First, have them tour your classroom. You probably have textbooks and reference books there along with a globe or atlas, a dictionary, and encyclopedias. Next, have students take a field trip to the school or community library. The librarians can explain to them what resources are available and how librarians can help them find exactly what they need.

Create a Museum That Shows Change Over Time

Break your class into small groups and assign each group a different social studies topic. Have each group create a "museum" of photographs and artifacts that reflect how that topic has changed over time. Topics could focus on transportation (e.g., Model T to present-day hybrid cars; canoes to cruise lines), technology (e.g., phonograph to MP3 players; typewriters to computers) or clothing (e.g., women's or men's fashion in the United States), just to give a few examples.

Use Visual Tools to Learn About Geographic Features

Graphic organizers offer a fun and visual alternative to give social studies lessons. Have your students use the wheel diagram on page 113 of this book to list Earth's five oceans. They can use the comparing two sides diagram on page 109 to list the features and purposes of the equator and the Prime Meridian. Try assigning them to take the world map on page 111 and label Earth's seven continents, five oceans, the equator, and the Prime Meridian.

Project-Based Learning

Learn More About Specific Cultures

Individually or in small groups, have students choose a specific cultural group to research. Cultural groups can be from the past, such as various American Indian tribes of North America. They could also be current-day groups such as the Amish or Cajun, or Japanese or Mexican. After researching, students should create a tool, doll, recipe, shelter, or other product that represents the culture. Allow students to share their research in a show-and-tell session.

Make an Interesting Presentation About an Indian Group

Guide students while they design a multi-media presentation about a specific American Indian culture. They should include information about food, clothing, language, shelter, and artistic expression. Encourage students to include visuals in their presentations. Help students draw inferences about how the physical environment influenced the culture, including the way people meet their needs.

Put Students in the Shoes of Your State's First Settlers

Tell your students to imagine they are new settlers in your state hundreds of years ago. Your students arrive with a few basic tools, some seeds, and a winter coat. They must build shelters. They must find water, hunt for food, and grow food. They have little or no medicine. They have no electricity. How do they build a city? Divide your class into two teams and come up with strategies to conquer this new land! Start with Week One, Week Two, etc.

Use Visual Tools to Learn About History

Graphic organizers offer a fun and visual alternative to give social studies lessons. Have your students use the buckets diagram on page 112 of this book to list features of personal communication and of mass communication. Direct them to use the steps diagram on page 110 to list important events of of a famous person's life.

Project-Based Learning

Create a Human Timeline

Have students create a human timeline to show the life of a famous person. Hand out cards with dated events on them, and tell students to organize themselves in chronological order.

Explore How Science and Technology Shaped History

Let students work together to create multimedia presentations that describe how science and technology have changed communication and travel over time. Discuss how advances in science and technology have changed our daily lives.

Science and technology examples might include:

- early flying machines to jumbo jets

- books to e-readers

- radios to MP3 players

- wall-mounted rotary phones to cell phones

- Model T to present-day hybrid cars

- canoes to cargo ships

Role-Play to Learn About How Elections Are Run

A great way to help your students learn about our leaders, including the president, governor, and mayors, is to let them have their own elections. Divide your students into small groups, preferably with an odd number of students in each group. These small groups represent cities. Have each small group nominate and then vote for their mayor. Explain to them the process as they do it. Combine the small groups into two or three larger groups. They are to maintain the integrity of their "city" group but they are also a part of a larger "state" group. Have each state elect a governor. Finally, have the whole class "country" nominate and vote on candidates for president.

Get Students Involved in Community Service

Ask each of your students to volunteer in some community activity and then report back to the class on what they did, how they helped, and how volunteering made them feel. Or, have students promote the common good by helping other students in their class or in the lower grades. Ideas for participation include tutoring, reading aloud, or creating and performing a skit about civic responsibilities.

Bring Economics Down to a Practical Level

Kids are consumers. They are often consumed with the problem of wants vs. needs. Making economic choices, especially saving first and then spending, are important skills for young people to learn.

Scarcity is not being able to have what we want because the supply doesn't meet the need. There are different ways to allocate scarce goods, including prices, command, first-come first-served, sharing equally, rationing, and lottery.

• Bring three popular music CDs into the classroom. Ask who wants them, and watch the hands go up! Try several methods to teach students about the pros and cons of allocation! Here is an idea:

• Tell students to line up in the order they returned to the classroom from lunch. Make them wait in line for 10 minutes. Then, give the CDs to the first three students in line.

* Was it worth the time spent waiting to get nothing?
* Would you wait in line again, knowing what you know now?
* Would you care enough to arrive in line early?

Make Economic Decisions in the Marketplace

Have two or three of your classes create and make a product (e.g., food, bookmarks, beaded bracelets). Then distribute a small amount of pretend money to each student to spend as each class sells their items (perhaps during lunch). Each student has the opportunity to be a producer by making a product, and a consumer by buying items.

VOCABULARY (side 1)

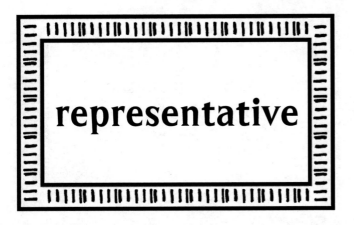

representative

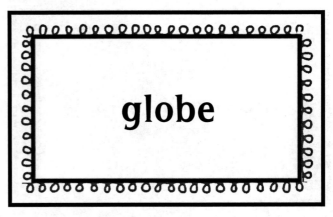

globe

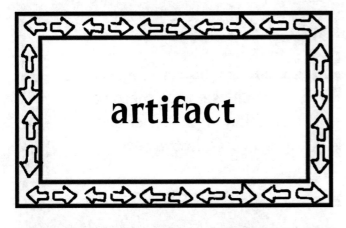

primary source

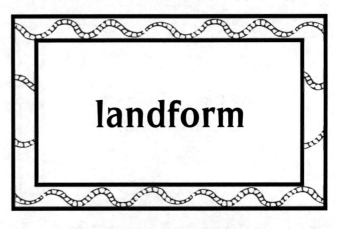

map

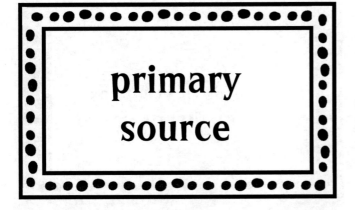

artifact

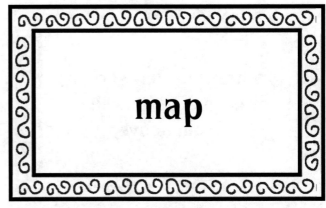

landform

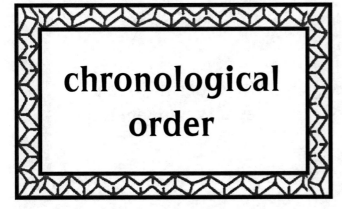

chronological order

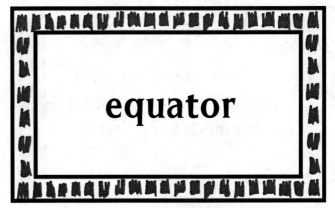

equator

VOCABULARY (side 2)

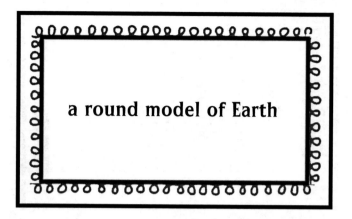
a round model of Earth

a person chosen to speak or act for others

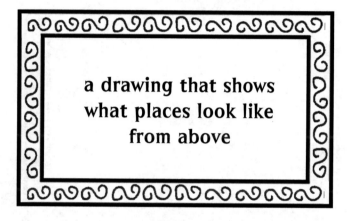
a drawing that shows what places look like from above

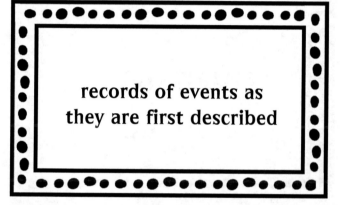
records of events as they are first described

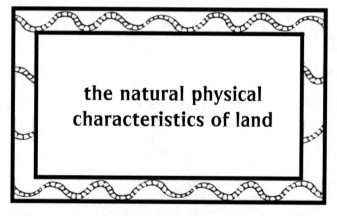
the natural physical characteristics of land

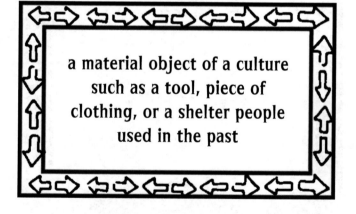
a material object of a culture such as a tool, piece of clothing, or a shelter people used in the past

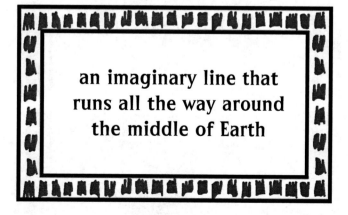
an imaginary line that runs all the way around the middle of Earth

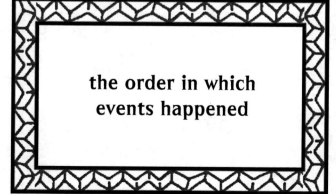
the order in which events happened

VOCABULARY (side 1)

Prime Meridian

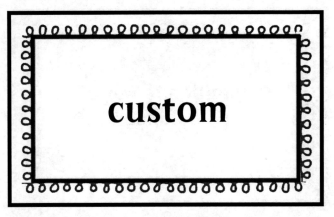

custom

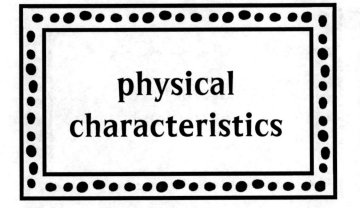

physical characteristics

community

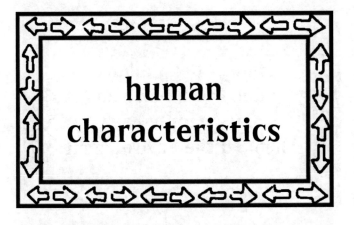

human characteristics

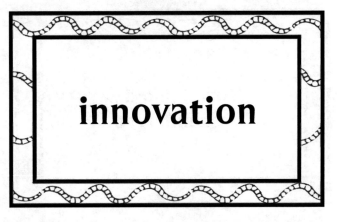

innovation

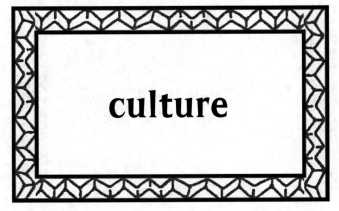

culture

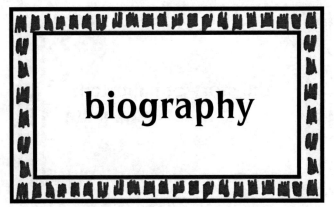

biography

VOCABULARY (side 2)

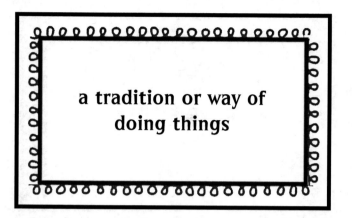

a tradition or way of
doing things

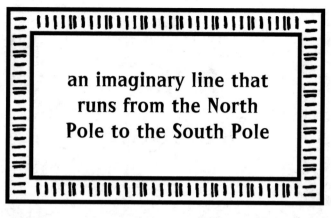

an imaginary line that
runs from the North
Pole to the South Pole

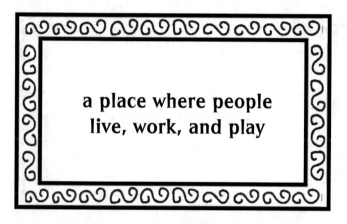

a place where people
live, work, and play

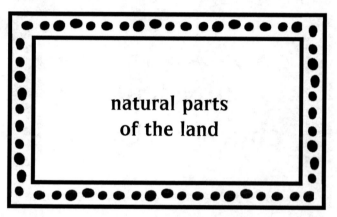

natural parts
of the land

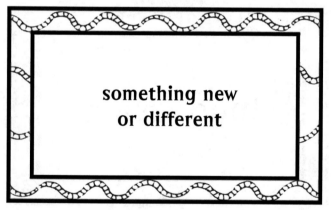

something new
or different

things people have
added to a place and
ways people have
changed the environment

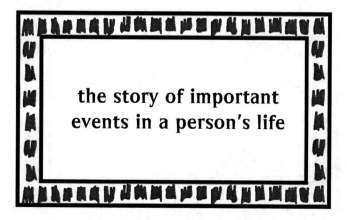

the story of important
events in a person's life

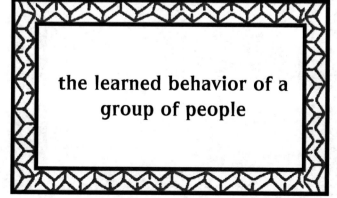

the learned behavior of a
group of people

VOCABULARY (side 1)

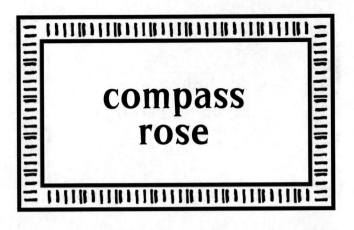

compass rose

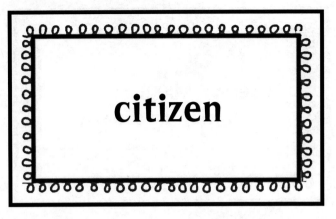

citizen

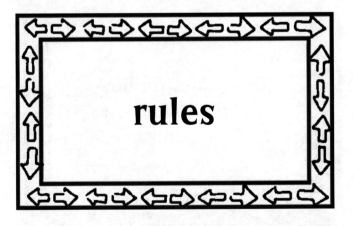

government

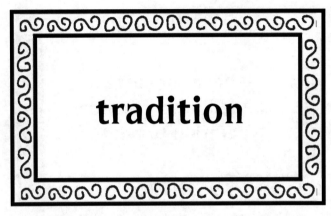

tradition

rules

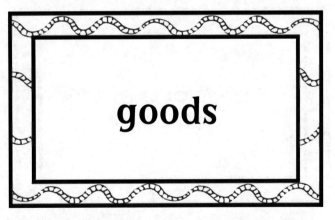

goods

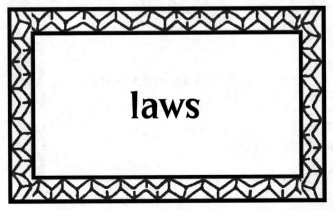

laws

services

VOCABULARY (side 2)

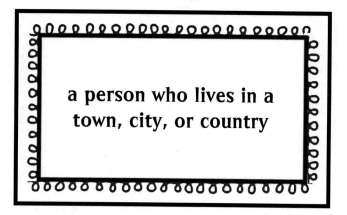
a person who lives in a town, city, or country

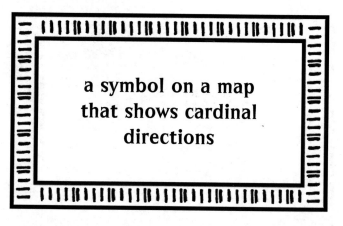
a symbol on a map that shows cardinal directions

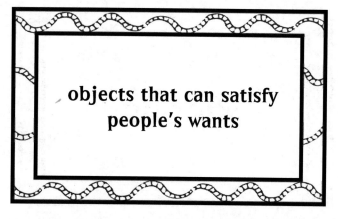
a belief or custom handed down from one generation to another

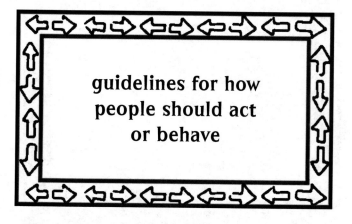
a group of people who make laws, carry out laws, and decide if laws have been broken

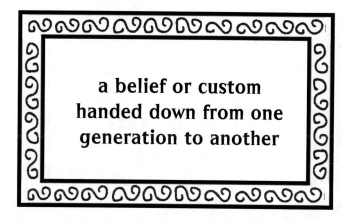
objects that can satisfy people's wants

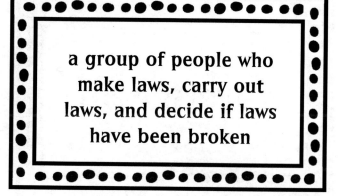
guidelines for how people should act or behave

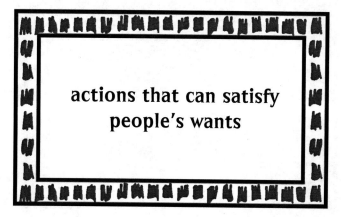
actions that can satisfy people's wants

official rules made and enforced by the government